Confronting
Without Guilt or Conflict

How to Prepare and Deliver a Confrontation
in a Way That Minimizes Risk, Conflict, and Guilt

Bob Weyant

Bob Weyant & Associates
P.O. Box 6414
Bellevue, WA 98008-0414

(425) 747-4898 • Fax: (425) 747-0724

First Edition

Bellevue, Washington

Confronting
Without Guilt or Conflict

How to Prepare and Deliver a Confrontation
in a Way That Minimizes Risk, Conflict, and Guilt

Bob Weyant

Published by:

PO Box 6414
Bellevue, WA 98008-0414 U.S.A

Copyright © 1994 by Robert F. Weyant
Fourth Printing 2000
Printed in the United States of America

Library of Congress Catalog Card Number: 94-96630
ISBN 0-9642576-5-3 Softcover

This book is dedicated to all the people in my life who challenged me to reach for the dreams I thought impossible.

And to Carol, who always knew I could and would.

Contents

Preface

I have written this book because the people I have worked with over the past 25 years have requested, even demanded it! I've been fortunate enough to have been pushed to provide effective life options by people who want to grow and want out of life and relationships everything that's possible! They have refused to settle for what is, the status quo.

As I have attempted to respond with skill development workshops, interventions, and written materials, they have wanted more. Of all the skills that people have wanted, this area of confronting and resolving conflicts, pro-actively, without conflict or guilt, is most in demand.

This book has evolved because people have not been able to find effective options to use to be as healthy and in control of their lives as they would like.

It is for anyone who wants to have effective options to be able to effectively deal with issues in any relationship. It is especially for people who have the following values:

- want to have control of their lives
- want openness and honesty in relationships
- believe in treating people with respect and compassion
- believe in dealing directly with issues
- believe that people should be accountable
- believe that people are responsible for their own lives

Influencing people is influencing people! The same skills used to influence a spouse or a friend are the same skills used to influence a boss or a peer. The options you have available to you are the same! You may choose a different option based on investment/ risk with a boss than with a peer or a friend, but the available options are the same.

The people who have requested this book have done so because they have found these skills to be relevant in business and at home. So use these skills in whatever role/ relationship you choose. You will find that, as you use the skills, they will begin to transfer to many interactions and relationships.

Yet these skills are not a cure-all for all situations. This book contains *suggested* options. There are no guaranteed, magic answers. Each human relationship and inter-action that is encountered is different and unique. There are a wide variety of interpersonal models and skills. The approach in this book is but one attempt to empower people to make meaning out of very complex processes of human relationships. Therefore, this approach is somewhat simplified. To be effective you should use your existing skills and use the skills contained in this book to complement them.

Examples from both business and personal life settings are used.

Although the confrontation skills you will learn apply to all relationships and interactions, they are especially relevant to important situations where you want to be more assertive or more in control of an emotional interaction than you have been in the past. Perhaps you have tried to resolve an issue several times with more collaborative strategies and nothing has worked. These skills enable you to take the risk to exert a higher level of control—not of people, but of the influencing process. You may feel that some of the options offered are too forceful, powerful, or controlling for your comfort. You alone have to decide for each relationship and situation how assertive you want to be. This Progressive Confrontation Model offers many options for the level of assertiveness, control, or collaboration you want to communicate.

Using the confrontation skills offered in this book can help minimize your feelings of guilt about the situation you are confronting. You will not have to feel guilty about hurting or devaluing the person you are confronting or for letting the confrontation deteriorate into a hurtful conflict.

It is not the goal of this book to address the larger life issue of dealing with guilt. Many of us have frequent feelings of guilt. Especially troubling are those times when these feelings do not seem warranted by the situation. It is my belief that these guilt feelings are often related to feelings of shame and are best explored in the context of your family of origin.

There are situations where these skills will probably not be successful. If you are dealing with an alcohol/drug abuser, a person who may be physically dangerous, or a person who is psychologically impaired, please seek professional help for workable options.

The sequence of this book is intended to help you develop a skill as you proceed through each of the chapters. Worksheets are provided at each step so you can develop and write a real confrontation for someone in your life. Additional copies of all worksheets are contained in Appendix B.

To whet your appetite and build a foundation of understanding for this new approach to confronting, Chapter 1 conceptually overviews the confrontation model and Chapters 2 through 5 provide the context of a broader influencing process.

Chapters 6 through 11 are the working sections: The Progressive Confrontation Model, Preparing for the Confrontation, Dealing with Difficult Emotional Reactions, Practicing Your Confrontation, Changing Behavior, and Bringing It Together.

At any point in your reading, if you'd like to review how an effective confrontation proceeds, turn to pages 103-111 for examples.

An additional Appendix, Confrontation for Supervisors, is included for those in a supervisory role.

An Index is provided in the back of the book to assist you.

Please note that throughout this book I have avoided gender-biased language by alternating male and female personal pronouns: he/him/his are used alternately with she/her/hers, and are intended to include both genders.

Many people have been instrumental in this book's development. Thanks to all my clients who asked me to write it, to all the effective people I've met who have modeled these skills without even realizing it, and to the many researchers and authors who have gone before. Dana Nunnelly's guidance, creativity, and flexibility were invaluable. I thank Robin Paris Hughes for her input, and Kris Fulsaas for her technical expertise and patience. Special thanks to Art O'Neal and Carolyn Wilken for their integrity and belief in these skills and their use in their organizations.

INTRODUCTION

Confrontation or Conflict?

Your Choice!

Confrontation

> *"To stand or **come in front of;** stand or meet facing.*
>
> *To face in hostility or defiance; oppose; to sit face-to-face.*
>
> ***To bring together for examination** or comparison."*
>
> —The New American College Dictionary

Conflict

> *"**To come into a collision,** clash, or to be in opposition or at variance.*
>
> *To contend; do battle."*
>
> —The New American College Dictionary

This book will teach you to *"**come in front of**"* another person and to *"**bring together to examine**"* any issue, especially those that you experience as risky or emotionally difficult.

We call this process confrontation and redefine it as a non-conflict model so that you can minimize the possibility of having *"**to come into a collision.**"*

My goal is to teach you how, when someone's behavior is causing you a problem, irrespective of his role, relationship with you, or position:

> **To go to the person immediately, in private, with respect, and request a change of behavior and come to some resolution without procrastinating, festering, losing sleep, or feeling guilty, and, most importantly, without conflict!**

If you want this skill, this book is for you!

Effective People

> **Effective people solve problems; ineffective people are unwilling to pay the price.**

Effective people, when they experience any problem in life, immediately address the issue. They perceive objectively first what the problem is and its causes, including their own behavior, and then what realistic options they have . . . they face reality!

Next, they make a choice. They consider what options they have to influence the external cause of the problem. These external options may be teaching, informing, problem solving, negotiating, or *confronting*. They then make a decision . . . is their investment to address the issue worth it or not? If it is, they begin their influencing process. If not, they accept it and let it go. In essence, they decide to increase (up) their level of control of the influencing process or to accept it and let it go.

This acceptance or "accepting it" process is not easy for most people. The very fact that we are emotionally hooked by an issue means that the issue is important to us, emotionally, spiritually, or at a deep value level. Accepting it means internally changing our value or expectation, a difficult task. Yet, when and if we truly "accept it," the same issue does not bother us nearly as much or cause the same emotional reaction. Accepting it does not mean that we agree, but that we have consciously decided to not let it bother us.

Ineffective People

Effective people do not remain ineffective and stay caught in the middle.

Ineffective people are unwilling to pay the price of taking control of their lives. They stay in a victim stance, agonizing, complaining, and finding someone to blame. The price to solve the problem, either outside of themselves (trying to influence the external cause) or inside themselves (acceptance), is too high! Dealing with problems is either an outside job or an inside job, it is not staying caught in the middle.

If someone's behavior is undesirable to you and causing you a problem and all the options you have applied to influence a change have not worked . . . try a new option! Don't continue to try the same thing and stay in the rut!

**Ineffective behavior is doing the same thing over and over again
and expecting different results each time.**

Confrontation is one of the key options that can empower you to take control of your life. But there is a price . . . there is always a risk!

The question is, do you want to take the risk to try to address the issue? Or do you want to take the risk of being a victim and perceiving yourself as powerless? *You do have options!*

CHAPTER 1

Confrontation: Our Current Dilemma

Confrontation. When you even think about initiating a confrontation, what thought, feeling, or reaction do you have? Apprehension? Fear? Flight? Anger? Avoidance? If you are like most people, your reaction is probably negative!

There is a tragic but very good reason why we generally have this negative reaction. The experiences most of us have had, either confronting someone or being confronted, often have been negative, hurtful, volatile, emotional, devaluing, and out of control, and have usually made our relationship with the other person worse!

Why? Because no one has taught us to confront effectively, with respect. It's not a skill that's generally taught in schools or families or businesses.

Not Confronting Often Makes It Worse

Where does not having an effective confrontation option leave us? In avoidance, procrastination, denial, and powerlessness. We put off the confrontation because, given our lack of know-how, to confront will make it worse!

Yet if we don't confront, we have a dilemma, a classic "between a rock and a hard place." If we can't confront we stay frustrated and resentful, have lowered productivity, and fester. In the meantime, the other person is going on her merry way. If we confront in an unskilled fashion, we risk causing a real conflict, harming the relationship, and feeling bad, even guilty.

If we don't confront, what happens to our frustration and resentment? Many people admit that they relieve this distress by talking about the person to others, complaining, judging, and gossiping. When we get temporary relief this way, we know that we are not being effective and respectful, and so feel guilty. So if we continue in this dilemma, what happens? If we don't confront, the other person continues the undesirable behavior and gets better at it. Whenever, and if, we do confront, the longer we have put it off, the more invested the other person will be in his behavior, and the tougher the confrontation will be.

He will be more practiced! We will be more resentful! A deadly combination that often results in a potentially volatile, out-of-control interaction!

As we put off the confrontation and try to avoid it, there will be a day when perhaps we're tired, stressed, moody, or not on guard, and the person will once again exhibit the undesirable behavior. It *will* happen, it's just a matter of time. It will be the proverbial last straw. At that point, we will react and probably be out of control, emotional, and hurtful, and the outburst will harm the relationship! Both parties will probably end up being defensive, thus not engaging in problem solving.

We have a million excuses that we use to avoid a confrontation:

> *"It's not my role."*
>
> *"Someone else will tell them."*
>
> *"Maybe I'm too critical."*
>
> *"They're having a bad day . . . it will get better."*
>
> *"It will hurt them."*

Often this conscious avoidance of confrontation is due to lack of skill or confidence. Other times the avoidance is subconscious and is some form of denial; it helps us avoid the reality that the person's behavior is causing a problem, that it's undesirable, that we don't know how to deal with it effectively, and that, unless it's addressed, it will probably continue. In fact, the other person probably doesn't even know that her behavior is a problem—how could she? I've not confronted her!

In my work, teaching and facilitating people to do confrontations, I have observed that approximately 50 percent of the time the person confronted was not aware that his behavior was a problem. A great majority of our behaviors are habits and are, therefore, beyond our conscious awareness—they are blind spots to us!

Redefining Confrontation Opens New Options

So, is there any doubt why we should be able to confront effectively? It is a fact that, as we proceed through this life, other people's behavior will cause us problems. People are not necessarily bad or wrong, just unique. Because they are different, their behavior will at times not meet our expectations. At any point, if their behavior causes us a problem or is undesirable to us, we have an opportunity to confront. We may choose not to because it is not worth the investment or risk. *But, if the behavior is a problem and is worth addressing, we need to confront and do it effectively.* But without guilt or conflict!

What are the benefits of effective confrontation? If we do confront effectively:
- We take control of our life.
- We avoid being in a victim stance.
- We improve our stress levels and mental health by avoiding the festering.
- We don't build up emotional baggage that will betray us when we do confront.
- We invest in a relationship in a positive way.
- We can be helpful to another person.

*And **what are the negative consequences of not confronting or of confronting ineffectively?*** If we do not confront and/or don't "accept it and let it go":
- We are not in control of our life.
- We increase our stress and our own mental health deteriorates.
- We build and carry emotional baggage, i.e., we fester.
- We harm the relationship with the other person by detaching or by being judgmental or resentful.
- We enable the other person to continue an undesirable behavior that may have negative consequences to him or to others.

Let's look at confrontation from a more personal angle. Imagine that your behavior is causing someone else a problem. Do you want her to talk behind your back; fester and dislike you or hold a grudge; be critical of you without requesting, specifically, what she wants?

Most of us would like the person to come to us with respect and confront the issue without being hurtful or devaluing.

Avoiding the confrontation means "we don't care enough to invest." Yet, if we don't know how to confront, we won't do it.

Confronting, then, if done effectively, can be a very caring gesture.

How do we confront effectively? First, let's get clear about the goal of confronting and redefine confrontation as a non-conflict process.

Confrontation Is a Request for Behavior or Behavior Change

Confrontation is a matter of going to the person and requesting what you want.

Think about it. Since another person's behavior is causing you a problem (is undesirable to you), you have two basic options to use to address the issue:

1. Tell the person what behavior is undesirable to you.

2. Tell the person what behavior you want, that if done, will resolve the issue and make the relationship better.

The Characteristics of Ineffective Confrontation

The typical confrontation, the one that is hurtful and, thus, the one we avoid, addresses the undesirable behavior. If we approach the confrontation by addressing the undesirable behavior, there are predictable, negative consequences caused by the characteristics of ineffective confrontation, such as:

• the expression of excessive "emotional baggage," like anger,

• using "blaming you,"

• describing the undesirable behavior, and/or

• describing the negative consequences that have resulted from the undesirable behavior.

Typically, when we confront ineffectively, it's because we have reacted. Previously, we put off the confrontation and built some emotional "steam." Then, we "blew"! Here are examples of ineffective confrontation:

(Angrily): *"You really hurt me! Last night when you finished your work, you just left without even offering to help! You are so insensitive! At times I don't think you care about anyone else, just yourself! And you expect people to help you! Not any more!"*

(Annoyed, but trying to be polite): *"Why did you leave so hurriedly last night?"*

Notice the negative emotional tone, the "blaming you," the dwelling on the undesirable behavior and the negative consequences ("*. . . you expect people to help you. Not any more!*").

Any one of these ingredients has a high probability of causing defensiveness in other people. They react, defend, withdraw, attack, or whatever. Now we have exactly the type of interaction that we wanted to avoid. Even more tragic. When we're done, *they still don't know what we want—we haven't told them!* All we have done is purge our emotions and resentments and harm the relationship.

No wonder we avoid confrontation! *A majority of typical confrontations are hit and run!*

Over the past few years, many trainers and consultants have taught, and continue to teach, people to confront as follows:

> *"I was really disappointed when you left work last night without checking with me to see if I needed help. It made me feel that you don't care."*

Notice the same ineffective confrontation characteristics of focusing on undesirable behavior, focusing on the "blaming you," and focusing on negative consequences.

Characteristics of Effective Confrontation

This book teaches a much more effective, non-harmful, non-conflict way to confront! An easier, softer way! It is based on requesting what you want, instead of devaluing and dwelling on what you don't like. It requires a mind-set that says this moment is the first moment of the rest of your life and the relationship with this person. After all, she can't do anything about what she has done in the past. You can only try to *influence* her behavior from this moment on, and she can only *change* her behavior from this moment on.

These are the characteristics of effective confrontation:

- uses no excess emotional baggage (calm, rational, respectful)
- requests the desired behavior
- describes the positive consequences if the person demonstrates the desired behavior
- uses "I" messages and, thereby, avoids the "blaming you"

Here's a comparison of ineffective and effective confrontation using the same example from above:

> Ineffective: *"I was really disappointed when you left work last night without checking with me to see if I needed help. It made me feel that you don't care."*

> Effective (calmly, with focus and confidence): *"I would like you to be more supportive of me. For example, before leaving work, check with me to see if I need help and, during the day, if I look stressed offer to help without me having to ask. As a result, I will feel that you care and be more productive and more willing to help you."*

Notice that being calm gets rid of the emotional tension, requesting the desirable behaviors avoids focusing on undesirable behaviors, describing the positive consequences avoids the threat of negative consequences, and giving an "I" message avoids using the "blaming you."

Using this approach, *you* have eliminated as many of the characteristics as possible that "tweak" defensiveness.

There is always a risk to any confrontation—there is no such thing as a no-risk confrontation for two reasons:

1. There is always an implication that the person has done something undesirable from your point of view (why else would you be asking for a change?).
2. People may react emotionally or defensively, by habit, in any number of ways irrespective of how effective you are. You are ultimately powerless over their reaction. You can only be respectful and avoid devaluing or hurting them.

Confrontation Is a Three-Part Process

Begin thinking of the confrontation process as a three-part process, each of which, if you are to be effective, requires several skills:

- **Share Your Expectations:** Send or articulate the issue specifically and in a way that lessens the chance of defensiveness—if you don't tell the person specifically what you want, she doesn't know what you want.
- **Perceive the Other Person's Response:** Perceive whether you're getting a "yes" or a "no."
- **Deal With the Other Person's Response:** Deal with the other person's reaction in a way that does not allow conflict, loss of control, or emotional hurt.

Progressive Confrontation Options

This new redefined Progressive Confrontation Model provides three options for requesting a behavior change. These options allow you to confront based on the level of assertiveness and importance you want to communicate or the level of control of the influencing process you want to maintain. The three Progressive Confrontation Options are:

- **Discrepancy Confrontation:** A soft, low-risk option that invites the other person to dialogue and discuss the issue.

- **Behavior Request Confrontation:** The most frequently used option that is direct, but is delivered in a way that lessens or eliminates defensiveness.

- **Accountability Confrontation:** An option that firmly but respectfully brings an issue "to a head" and forces a clear "yes" or "no" from the other person.

Confrontation is necessary, but not enough. Making the confrontation only starts the process! Dealing with the reaction and following up is critical!

I find it very difficult to imagine going through life without having the option to confront when I need to and choose to.

> ## Confrontation is a primary human influencing option!

Now you have an overview of this new, non-conflict model. Remember, confrontation is one of several options and part of a more generic influencing process, which is covered in Chapters 2 through 5. Chapter 6 describes confrontation options. Chapters 7 through 10 will help you prepare and practice your confrontation and Chapter 11 offers two sample confrontations.

CHAPTER 2

The Influencing Process

You are in the influencing business, whether you want to be or not!

*Influencing: To be able to get people to do what you want them to do, preferably because they choose to and not because they are forced to, and to do it in a way that their defensiveness goes down (***D↘***) and their trust of you goes up (***T↗***).*

Whether you're aware of it or not, you are in the influencing business. When you get up in the morning and proceed through the world, you need to be able to influence people to do the things you need or want them to do. There is not anyone who doesn't need to influence at least one person during the day:

- You need your partner to be nice.
- You want your kids to hear correctly.
- You want your colleagues to be helpful.
- You want your friend to be open and tell you how his day went.
- You want someone who is frustrating you to change her behavior.

Your behavior influences, not your intentions.

Many of us are not aware that we are influencing people all of the time! We may not purposefully intend to or even be aware that we are, but we are!

Remember the last time a family member came home in sort of a bad mood, with a frown, lowered energy, or tension. She may not have intended to influence you negatively, but she did. You tensed up, became concerned, wondered if it was something you did (took it personally). Her intentions were different than her behavior, but it was her behavior that influenced (caused) your negative reaction.

Perhaps she had a bad, stressful experience and fully intended to "leave it" at work or school. She did not want to negatively affect you, but her behavior did! She probably was not even aware that she looked stressed and droopy or that it influenced you.

On the other hand, think of a person who is always positive and pleasant. When she is around, you feel better and more positive too. She is probably not trying to influence you or is not aware that she is, but she is!

Most of us are really good, respectful, caring people who intend to portray the same. Yet, due to moods and habits, many of which we are unaware of, our *"outside"* behavior does not represent our *"inside"* intentions.

> **We are responsible for our behavior.**
> **Our intentions never influenced anyone.**

I often hear people say *"I didn't mean that"* or *"They didn't understand what I meant"* or *"That's not what I intended,"* yet it is the behavior—specifically the words, posture, facial expression, and tone of voice—that caused the reaction. Our behavior shouldn't be an excuse!

Remember: We are always influencing, irrespective of our role at the moment, and it's our behavior that has consequences.

> **Effective people are aware of their behavior and its consequences,**
> **and continually strive to do better!**

Frame of Reference

All of your influencing is based on your perceptions of the world. Your view of the world is based on your frame of reference. Your frame of reference is the sum total of all of your life experiences, your beliefs, values, feelings, and thoughts. As you go through life, each experience is filtered through this frame of reference. You have heard the saying "You hear what you want to hear." It is not totally true, but because we filter what we experience, we often do distort reality. Our perception is often different from reality.

It is important to keep in mind, as you consider confronting a person, that your perception of the situation is based on your frame of reference and the situation may be perceived differently by the other person. There may be another view, another side of the story, or a different conclusion.

Thus, all influencing, including confrontation, should be considered a process. You start the process from your point of view (frame of reference), fully understanding that you may get a different view from the other person.

Rarely is good communication a defense of one's frame of reference.

People who are effective at the influencing process find it very, very easy, uncomplicated, and efficient. If you *are* good at influencing, you make a low investment of time and energy, and get a high return. People generally do what you want them to. If you're *not* good at this influencing process, it takes too much time and energy, it's emotional, and people don't do what you want.

There is a basic process that underlies a great majority of the influencing that we do, whether it be confronting, negotiating, teaching, or informing. It's like the DNA molecule in your body. You may not be aware of the molecule and how it works, but it is working constantly and is the basis of all your functioning. By understanding its functioning, you can understand the more complex physiological processes. The same is true in influencing. If you understand the basic process, you will more easily understand the more complex processes like confrontation.

If you can *influence effectively*, the people you are influencing probably:

1. understand, specifically, what you want or need, and
2. listen and are open to being influenced because your process results in their defensiveness going down and their trust going up (**D↘T↗**).

If you are *not effective at this influencing process*, people probably:

1. do not know what you want and then have to guess or ask, and/or
2. because of your process, they are defensive (**D↗T↘**), reactive, not open, and basically, at the moment, "closed."

Because I believe so strongly that you need to be effective at influencing and that your effectiveness is determined by your choosing options based on an analysis of investment versus return, I call this effective influencing process *Low-Investment/High-Return Influencing*.

How High-Return Influencing Works

Remember, influencing means to be able to get people to do what you want them to and to do it in a way so that their defensiveness goes down and their trust of you goes up (**D↘T↗**).

If you are *effective*, the process is cost effective and efficient, i.e., a small amount of time is required, you stay focused on the issue, and the relationship is improved (**D↘T↗**). Influencing usually becomes easier with this person the next time.

If you are *not effective*, the process is costly and inefficient, i.e., it takes too much time, does not stay on the desired issue, and deteriorates the relationship (**D↗T↘**). Influencing usually becomes more difficult with this person the next time.

The more effective you are at this influencing process with any one person, the easier it becomes in the next interaction with him.

> **Every time you interact with a person you're either improving the relationship or making it worse.**

Trust Meter Analogy

A critical part of your ability to influence any person is the amount of trust you have built in that specific relationship.

The extent of this trust is earned and based on how you have treated this person in all past interactions. If you have treated him well, e.g., respectfully, honestly, or supportively, he probably trusts you and your process (**D↘T↗**). You have credibility and influence and what will later be called "personal power" with him.

If you have not treated this person well, e.g., been disrespectful, dishonest, or unsupportive, he probably doesn't trust you or your process (**D↗T↘**) and you lack credibility and influence. You may not have intended to have these negative consequences or even be aware that you have had them.

Imagine that every person with whom you interact has a circuit panel in his body and that in this panel are small meters or gauges, each with a needle that registers trust of a person. The trust reading at any moment is cumulative and based on all of your past behavior with him. That person has a trust meter with your name on it!

Trust Meter

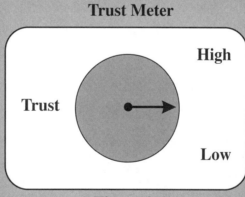

Figure 2-1

If his trust-meter reading for you is high, your influence is higher and much easier and he most likely will "give you the benefit of the doubt."

If his trust-meter reading for you is low, you've got a real problem in this relationship!

The "influencing process," as was introduced in Chapter 1, is a three-step process, each step of which involves key skills (Figure 2-2):

    1. Step One - Share Your Expectations (Tell Others What You Want)

    2. Step Two - Perceive the Other Person's Response

    3. Step Three - Deal With the Other Person's Response

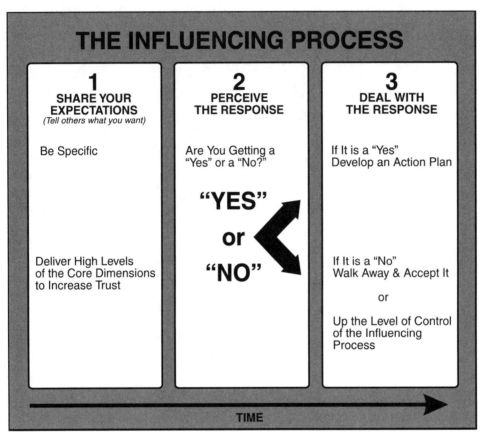

Figure 2-2

The key skills for Step One, *Share Your Expectations*, are to be able to:

- Tell others specifically what you want.
- Articulate in a way that lessens defensiveness and increases trust (**D↘T↗**) by delivering a high level of the Core Dimensions of Human Nourishment. These Core Dimensions are respect, empathy, specificity, and genuineness and are fully defined in Chapter 3, Share Your Expectations.

The key skill to Step Two, *Perceive the Response*, is being able to perceive whether you are getting a clear "yes" or a "no."

The key skills to Step Three, *Deal With the Response*, are to be able to:

- Get a commitment to a verbal "yes."

- Have effective options, if you get a "no," to influence the response toward a "yes."

We are describing here a *process* and not a "cookbook," cause-and-effect, linear, guaranteed set of techniques. A process means that you have a starting point and then, as you begin, you will get more "data"—the other person's reaction and view from her frame of reference. As you perceive the new data (perceive reality), based on a cost/benefit analysis of several possible options, you choose the option that enables you to continue to move toward your goal. This process means that you start with clarity about what you want and articulate your issue specifically and in a way that increases trust and lessens defensiveness. From this point on, you have no control over the other person or her reaction. You *can* have control of the influencing process. The very act of starting the process will influence some reaction or new data. When you use a *technique*, you use an automatic next step irrespective of what data or reaction you get. When you use a *skill*, you incorporate the new data and choose from options.

> **Effective people perceive reality and have options.**

Keeping control of the influencing process means that you keep the interaction:

1. on the relevant issue (usually yours);

2. respectful and not hurtful and/or emotionally out of control; and

3. moving toward a clear "yes" or a clear "no."

Losing control of the influencing process means that you have allowed the interaction to:

1. get off the relevant issue (yours);

2. become disrespectful and hurtful and/or emotionally out of control; and/or

3. not move toward a clear "yes" or a clear "no."

**We are powerless over people,
but can be in control of the influencing process.**

Keeping control of the process requires a number of skills that you may use as options as the interaction proceeds. At each step you have choices regarding whether you invest further and what skill to use. I offer *no* magic "if you do this, this will happen" techniques. Each of us, as we interact, may choose different options, different investments of time and risk, a different pace, and a different willingness to accept certain consequences. At each point in an interaction you have options to "up the level of control" of the influencing process or to walk away (accept it) and let it go.

**There is no right or wrong to this influencing process,
just options consistent with your values.**

As you interact with people many times a day, you don't need help with those interactions that are respectful and are getting you what you want ("yeses"). Where you would probably like help is in dealing with interactions where you are not being successful getting a "yes" and/or where the interaction is emotional, risky, and volatile. The greatest benefit for using the skills in this book is with these tough interactions. *The key is to be able to keep control of the influencing process!* (See Chapter 5, Deal With the Response and Keep Control of the Process.)

When you encounter these more difficult interactions, it is important that you have the skill to "up the level of control" of the influencing process.

Control is assertiveness, urgency, importance, and focus on a single issue. Upping your level of control means then that you increase the importance or urgency of your request. You're always communicating some level of control when you talk to people. Conversely, you're also communicating that they have some *choice* to say "no." People perceive your level of control and their level of choice, and prioritize the importance of what you're saying based on that data. It usually comes in your voice tone, your words, and your posture. Often, when you get a "no," the urge is to immediately move to a very high level of control, like threats, a loud voice, or the use of position power. Using the progressive confrontation options described in Chapter 6 allow you to more gradually increase your level of control.

Picture saying to your kids tonight, *"I would like you to think about maybe, possibly, perhaps considering, if you don't mind and it's not too much of a problem, maybe thinking about possibly taking the garbage out."* What's the probability of them doing it if you stated your request in this manner? Zero! How much control, importance, urgency, assertiveness was communicated? None. Inversely, then, how much choice did you tell them that they had to not do it? Lots. They would hear this choice and assume they don't have to do it. You need then, as you communicate, to understand what level of assertiveness/control you are exercising. Try to influence in a way that is soft and reasonable (low control/high choice), and if it works, fine, because it's not pushy. But if it doesn't work, you've got to have options to be able to up your level of control, if you choose.

Notice, using the last example, how the requests shown in Figure 2-3 (beginning from the bottom) communicate increasingly higher levels of control and, thus, lower levels of choice:

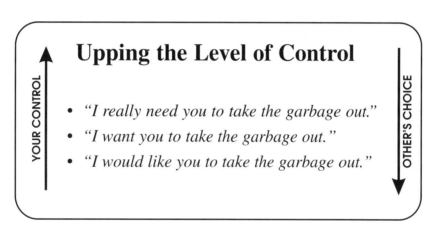

Figure 2-3

Now, taking the example a step further, you probably tried that lower level of control at some point, trying to be nice, polite, and not controlling or parental. You got a "no" and, without knowing this model at the time, you probably upped your level of control. At some point you said, *"You know, I would really like you to take the garbage out."* You still got a "no." *"I really need you to take this out."* Probably that didn't work. Probably every time you said, *"Look, the garbage is really important,"* that didn't work. You know what most of us would do with our kids at this point? We would walk in and say, *"Take the garbage out or else."* A very high level of control!

Let's take the example even further. Let's say you discipline your kids. Are your kids happy about that? Disciplining your kids—taking the TV away or grounding them—is upping your level of control to a very high level. Do you expect them to throw their arms around you and say, *"Oh, thanks. I really appreciate this. I need this."*? No. They are going to roll their eyes, not speak to you, give you the cold shoulder, and make you suffer for days. Their defensiveness goes up, their trust goes down. If you use this very high level of control, you should be willing to expect **D↗T↘**. Don't be surprised. Be willing to pay that price or don't do it. It is not right or wrong, it is a choice with consequences for each option.

The degree of control/choice communicated is neither right nor wrong. It is a way of choosing the degree of importance that you want to convey to a particular person on a particular issue. At a different time you might choose a different degree of control/choice.

The higher the level of control, the higher the risk (D↗T↘).

The generic *influencing process* involves three steps:
- Share your expectations.
- Perceive the other person's response.
- Deal with the other person's response.

CHAPTER 3

Share Your Expectations

As you have learned, the first step in effective influencing is to share your expectations. The two primary ingredients in sharing your expectations effectively are *to be specific* and *to deliver high levels of the Core Dimensions*.

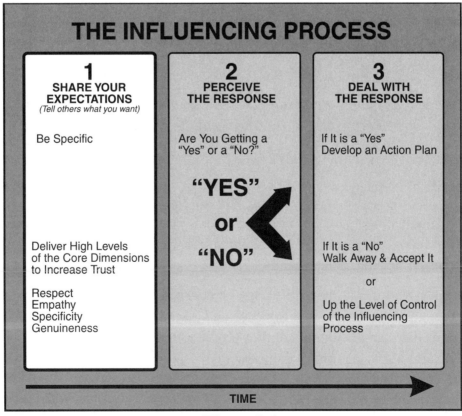

Figure 3-1

Be Specific

Tell the person what you want and *be specific*. To the degree the person does not know what you want, she either has to take the time to figure it out, or she has to guess. If she is guessing, she is probably going to guess wrong and maybe react negatively or do the wrong thing. You were not specific. Let's take an example: How specific is the following statement?

You say:

> *"Marcy, I need you, as we work together every day, to be more coopera-tive and supportive of me."*

As you try to determine whether this statement is specific, you may think "yes, it is" or "no" or "I'm not sure." Many people are not sure. Many of us do not have a model or paradigm for specificity. Let's take this sample interaction a bit further.

Marcy says:

> *"Sure, no problem, I would be glad to."*

She gave you a pretty clear "yes." You think you have an agreement and are relieved to not be in conflict.

Tomorrow at work she does not speak to you and, in fact, appears to be avoiding you. You are somewhat confused because this behavior contradicts her agreement. You decide after three days of the same non-cooperative behavior to up the level of control of the process and confront the issue. (You could have chosen to accept it, not invest, and walk away; remember, you do have options!)

You say:

> *"Marcy, I am confused, because on the one hand you said you would be more cooperative, while on the other hand I have not been spoken to for three days."*

Marcy says:

> *"Oh, but I have been cooperative. You are the one that complains more than anyone about having too much work to do, so I thought the most cooperative, supportive thing I could do would be to leave you alone so you might get your work done!"*

Marcy is right! You were not specific, so she guessed or interpreted what you meant. People guess based on their past experience and own unique frame of reference. Now you have a problem and potential conflict (**D↗T↘**) and, if nothing else, this influenc-ing process is taking more time and energy than you wanted.

Now, using the same example, let's be specific:

You say:

> *"Marcy, I would like you to be more cooperative and supportive of me as we work together every day; by that I mean, twice a day I want you to come to me without me asking and just check with me and ask if there is anything you can do to help me. If you see me running around confused, harried, or overwhelmed, I would like you to come and offer to help me. As a result, if you will do this, my productivity is going to go up and I will be a lot more willing to help you."*

Notice the difference. If you use words like "cooperative," "supportive," "timely," "accurate," "positive attitude," "be committed," "treat your mom with respect," you are not specific. Being specific is a skill most people need to learn. I work with people all over the country, from all walks of life, and, regardless of their education, vocation, or role, most have difficulty being specific, not in writing, but interpersonally. Learning to be specific and to perceive specificity is like having "an ear for music"; I would like you to develop an "ear for specificity."

Being specific is the key to influencing and, therefore, to confrontation.

Now you will recognize how the following request may cause you difficulty in your influencing process because of your lack of specificity:

> *"I would like you to clean up your room by the end of the weekend."*

What is *"clean"* and when is the *"end of the weekend?"*

This is not what was meant. The specific request should have been:

> *"I would like you to clean up your room by the end of the weekend, by that I mean by 4:30 p.m. Sunday, before dinner, without me having to remind you. Clean means all toys put away, bed sheets changed, the floor vacuumed, including under the furniture. If you do, you will be able to find your things and I won't bug you about not doing it."*

A friend reported that he requested that his daughter clean her room by the end of the weekend. She said, *"Sure, no problem."* He learned the hard way that the end of the weekend to her was 7:30 a.m. Monday morning *if* he caught her before she left for school. Clean to her meant that if you could walk through the center of the room it was OK. Specificity creates an entirely different message! Being specific takes care of the stating "what you want" part of the influencing process.

Deliver High Levels of the Core Dimensions

In addition to being specific about your expectations, it is imperative that you articulate them in a way that lessens defensiveness and increases trust (**D↘T↗**).

Researchers (R. R. Carkhuff and B. G. Berenson) have found that we are delivering—you and I and everyone in the world—some level of what are called the Core Dimensions of Human Nourishment (see Figure 3-1). We are delivering some level of these all of the time that we are awake. In fact, there is no such thing as not delivering the Core Dimensions. It's a matter of degree. These Core Dimensions that influence trust are *respect*, *empathy*, *specificity*, and *genuineness*. No matter what issue you're dealing with, if you deliver a high level of these Core Dimensions in that interaction, the probability is very high that the other person experiences the interaction pleasantly. Pleasantly (or at least not unpleasantly) means that his defensiveness goes down, his trust-meter reading goes up, and you have an open system that might be influenced. That's all you can ask. Do you realize you cannot make anybody *do* anything? All you can do is behave in a way that increases the probability of a person being open enough to being influenced and to give you a chance.

Now let's define the Core Dimensions:

Respect

Respect is non-judgmentalness. Respect means that your behavior sends a message that the other person is equal, valuable, and OK. Disrespect communicates that the other person is dumb, stupid, inferior, or less than you. We communicate low levels of respect—and, therefore, the probability of defensiveness going up, and trust going down (**D↗T↘**)—through our body language, words, or voice tone. For instance, a roll of the eyes or a judgmental term are disrespectful.

Empathy

Empathy means that you can show somebody you understand what she feels, not what she says. Empathy requires that you communicate to the person an understanding of where she is and what her experience is at the moment. Empathy requires that you use a feeling word that accurately describes the other person's feelings, such as, *"So, you're **frustrated** because you have been trying hard and I don't seem to understand that."*

Specificity

Specificity means you are specific. To the degree you have not been specific, people have to guess or assume what you mean. They begin to guess wrong, including guessing about your motives. If you are specific, even if the person doesn't like what you are saying, the person can trust that your outside words match your insides (what you mean), and that there is no hidden agenda or meaning.

Genuineness

Genuineness means that you are authentic. Genuineness means that you represent, on the outside, what is inside, that you are congruent. What you feel and think on the inside are consistent with what you say and do on the outside. Your insides and outsides are integrated and consistent.

We need to deliver a high level of these Core Dimensions in every interaction. Everything in this book, no matter what the skill—including confrontation—is based on delivering a high level of these Core Dimensions.

Remember, no matter how effective you are at this influencing process, the other person may be resistant to changing and may ultimately give you a "no." Getting a "no" is not the end of the world. You still have options for yourself.

The problem in influencing is not that you get a "no," but the hurtful, emotional interactions that are often caused by a low level of delivery of the Core Dimensions.

> **If you deliver a high level of the Core Dimensions,**
> **you will have done everything possible to lessen the probability**
> **of being hurtful and devaluing, and, thus,**
> **to have caused defensiveness and loss of trust (D↗T↘).**

Now that you have shared your expectations effectively by being specific and delivering a high level of the Core Dimensions, you need to be ready to objectively Perceive the Response.

CHAPTER 4

Perceive the Response:
Are You Getting a "Yes" or a "No?"

You have told the person specifically what you want and delivered a high level of the Core Dimensions. So, after you've sent your message, *you need to perceive the essence of the response, that is, whether you're getting a "yes" or a "no."*

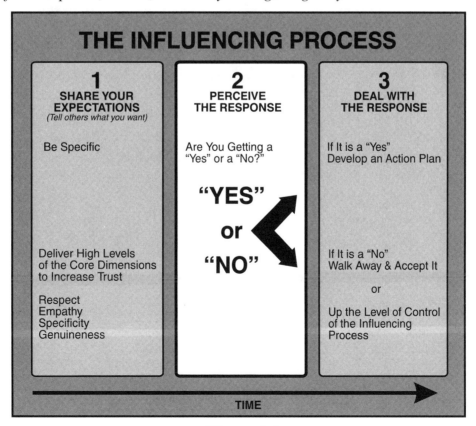

Figure 4-1

Rule of Thumb (you might try saying it out loud to yourself for practice!): *If I'm not getting a clear "yes" at the moment, I'm getting a "no" at the moment.*

Very simply, *the other person's behavior, at the moment,* is either a "yes" or a "no." What people say is only one behavior. Behavior also includes their voice tone, face, eyes, posture, gestures, and body language. It is important to consider their words, but their non-verbal behavior may be contrary evidence. Consider the whole package!

Stay out of the judgment business. A "no" is not right or wrong, good or bad. It's a piece of data. If you feel judgmental, you are reacting and will probably lose control of the process.

Stop-Sign Analogy

Let me offer an analogy about a "no." Imagine today that you're driving somewhere. Every stop sign you encounter is a "no." Don't go! Right? Everybody understands that. Now, think about all the types of stop signs. There's a little red sign. There's a solid red light. There's a blinking red light. It used to be that a yellow light meant stop. An officer with a flag is a "no."

You don't drive around saying, "Gee, I didn't see the stop sign." You see the "no" and you stop. You don't sit there and turn the car off forever because you come to a stop sign. You stop temporarily and you think, *"What are my options? When can I go? Is it safe to go? Do I go right or left?"*

Sometimes people's behavior can be a "no." It is important that you perceive that you are getting an "at-the-moment no" and that the form of the "no" does matter and should not confuse you. If you perceive it objectively, at the moment, *you have options.* At times not only do we not perceive the "no" objectively, but we even take it personally. We get angry and think thoughts like, *"Who the heck do they think they are?"*

Stop-Sign Analogy, *continued...*

Continue with your imaginary drive. As you come to a stop light or a stop sign, open your car door, get out, and start to scold the stop light. Say, *"You stupid stop light! Why did you make me stop?"* Go ahead and be judgmental of this "no." You'll probably get some very interesting reactions from the people who observe you!

We often get really judgmental of people when we get a "no." If so, we are not perceiving objectively, our rational brain is not engaged, and we are reactive. In this state of mind, our options are very limited. Any "no," irrespective of the kind of verbal or emotional behavior that accompanies it, is just a piece of data, just like a stop sign.

Even when you come to a stop sign out on the road, you don't have to stop forever. It's a temporary stop. You perceive the "no," honor it, consider options, and then go ahead toward your goal.

Smoke Screens

Given our new definition—*"if it's not a clear 'yes' at the moment, it's a 'no' at the moment"*—what are some behaviors that you've gotten or are getting that, by this definition, are "nos" or have some "no" in them?

> *"If I can." "I'll get back to you." "When I get around to it." "Perhaps." "Let me think about it." "Good idea."*

All of these responses have some "no" in them, although they are not intensely emotional or reactive. They are like yellow lights on the road. They've got some "yes," and they've got some "no." Try to consider what type of response you are getting based on the percentage of "yes" or "no" contained. Rarely are responses 100 percent "yes" or 100 percent "no." Most have some of each. And you've got choices: either take it as a "yes" and hit the gas pedal (go ahead), or take it as a "no" and hit the brake.

Many of us, especially when operating in the business world, are taught to not say flat "no" when responding to someone's request. It could be perceived as unwillingness, negativity, uncooperativeness, or insubordination. If we say "yes," we're untruthful because we don't mean it. If we say "no," we're going to be perceived as uncooperative, and that's really risky. What we've all learned, and every person does it, is to respond in some automatic verbal/emotional way that sort of camouflages the response. These "yellow-light" responses, which from now on are referred to as "smoke screens," are non-committal and buy us time to think. We are usually not even aware we are being unclear, and don't intend to be obstinate or evasive. But we all do it! Most "nos" are not permanent. They are just a reaction at the moment.

Saying "No" Effectively

If you're going to say "no," how do you do it effectively? It is very important that people in relationships be able to say "no." If they can't say "no," they either have to "fudge" and give a "yes" that really is a "no," or they give a smoke screen that wastes time and energy. I believe that it's really important to develop an agreement with your kids and others in your life that it's OK to say "no." To just say flat "no" by itself is not very effective. I'm suggesting that it is OK to say "no" if you do it in an effective, helpful manner.

A good way to say "no" is to say "no," and give the relevant reason. For instance, "No, I can't do it because I'm working on this and I thought it was a higher priority," then add, "I could help you later," or "Why don't you try so-and-so," or "If you'll help me with this, I can." So, give the "no" and the reason, and then help the person find an acceptable option.

It's OK to say "no" at the moment if you give the "because"; if it's a relevant, related reason; and if you help the person explore other options. A "no" by itself is not OK because it stops the process, unless you are willing to let the other person be in control!

Complaining, changing the subject, getting annoyed, questioning, being hurt, and technically dazzling with some knowledge are examples of these yellow-light type of smoke screens. We just react without forethought, using learned habits—every one of us has our own habits or smoke screens. You may ask questions or change the subject or get a little irritated or whatever it is and at the moment, since you are not giving a clear, 100 percent "yes," you are communicating some "no."

When you are influencing, dealing with these yellow lights ("nos") is relatively easy for two reasons: 1) They already have some "yes" in them; and 2) the person giving this type of response is usually not defensive. With this kind of "no" response, you typically either accept it as a "yes" or up your level of control and push (assert) for closer to 100 percent "yes."

The problem with these responses is also twofold: 1) We perceive them to be a 100 percent "yes," and when the person does not come through, we are surprised; and 2) we know we are getting a "no" and don't have an option to up the level of control to influence more "yes."

Occasionally, we encounter more than a yellow-light type of "no." The "no" is accompanied by much more emotion and reactiveness.

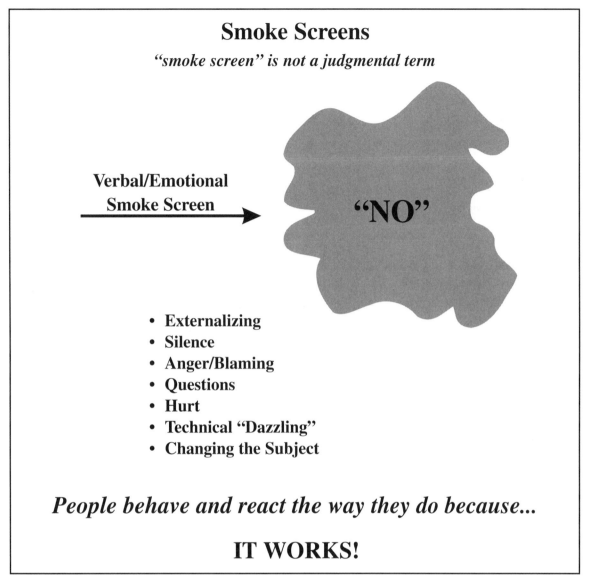

Figure 4-2

Emotional "Nos"

Most people have difficulty dealing with a "no" that has some substantial negative emotion attached, such as anger, defensiveness, accusation, or judgmentalness.

I'm sure that you have heard the phrase *"that sure pushed my button,"* meaning that you reacted in an emotional, not particularly rational or focused manner.

The problem with emotional "nos" is that the emotional part of the person's response pushes the older, reactive "fight or flight" part of your brain and, thus, circumvents the rational part of your brain that considers options: your cortex. At this point, instead of considering options and moving toward a "yes," you are probably arguing, defending, and dealing with issues other than your original request.

In *Dinosaur Brains*, A. J. Bernstein and Sydney Craft Rozen describe people who are overreacting as using their "dinosaur brain." A simplified version of the analogy may help to understand why we are so reactive.

Dinosaur Brain Analogy

Imagine an interaction between two dinosaurs. You have heard the old saying "fight or flight." These are the limited options dinosaurs had. Both options were losers in terms of resolving an issue. Either get in a conflict and get hurt or run and the issue was not resolved. In either case, the dinosaur just reacted emotionally for self-preservation and did not have the capability (cortex) to pause and think about options before acting.

We humans react the same way! We have that "dinosaur brain" buried in our "old brain" (physiologically true) and, if we don't override it with our cortex, we fight by getting angry, defensive, or devaluing or we take flight by being hurt, silent, or withdrawn. None of these reactive responses are usually effective.

Human beings have developed a cortex to enable us, before we react, to override our dinosaur brain and to formulate options. When we are ineffective it is often because we are reacting, not thinking. Effective people are able to override this old-brain reaction by using their cortex.

Getting Your Buttons Pushed

Who are the people in your life who really push your buttons and get at your emotional stuff? The people closest to you in your life—kids and often people of authority. A major focus of this book is to help you learn which buttons get pushed and to have some new responses so you do not have to respond from your dinosaur brain.

Each of us is unique in terms of what types of emotional responses push our buttons. Some of us respond defensively, while others "fold." What behaviors push your buttons? Crying? Anger? Intimidation? Whining?

People's responses and emotions may be very valid, but what is at the core of their response at the moment? A "no!" This verbal/emotional behavior is like *smoke*—not necessarily intentional, but there. No matter what verbal/emotional response you get, you should not let the smoke get in your eyes. You need to, with respect and compassion, stay on the issue and keep moving toward a "yes."

If you are good at dealing with "nos," especially emotional ones, you won't get sucked into an argument or a fight or get off the issue. You won't get intimidated and fold your tent and retract your offer. Effectively dealing with "nos" is sticking with the issue and moving it toward a "yes" without getting in a big emotional fight.

Up to this point you have learned to:

• Share your expectations specifically and with a high level of delivery of the Core Dimensions.

• Perceive to what degree you are getting either a "yes" or a "no" and not be confused by verbal/emotional smoke screens.

Now you need to be ready to deal with the response.

CHAPTER 5

Deal With the Response & Keep Control of the Process

Now that you have clearly discerned whether you are getting a "yes" or a "no," you have to have effective options for dealing with both.

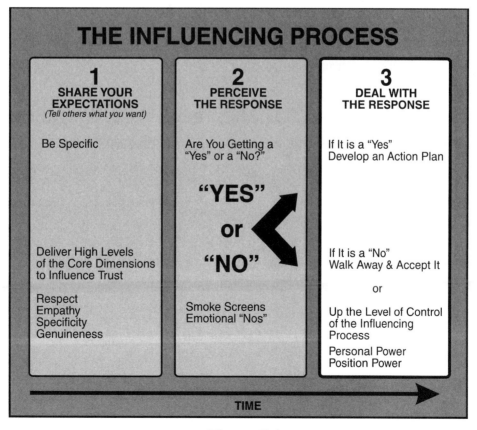

Figure 5-1

Have you ever had a person give you a "yes" and then not do it? What you got was a verbal "yes" then a behavioral "no." Did you get a little upset? If a person is going to give you a "yes" and not do it, would you like to know now, instead of a week from now? Sometimes you need to get a commitment right at the moment, to pin down the "yes" so it has a higher probability of happening, to increase the chance that this verbal "yes" will truly become a behavioral "yes." Following are some guidelines.

"Easy Yeses"

Do you consider yourself to be a cooperative, helpful, supportive person? Probably yes! Most of us are well-meaning people, and when somebody asks us to do something, we will say "yes" without even thinking, because we're automatically cooperative. We're giving an "easy yes" without thinking about what really will be required.

Envision the following interaction. You make a request of a colleague to compile a report by next Friday at noon, and he, being a nice, helpful person and without thinking, automatically says, *"Sure, no problem."* As soon as he walks away, he starts thinking, *"Oh, no. Why did I agree to that? I've got this training, I'm going to a workshop tomorrow, I've got parent/teacher conferences Thursday, I'm taking Monday off, I've got this big project—oh, wow!"*

So, his "easy yes" starts turning into a "no." But you think you got a "yes!"

Now, if you ask people to do something, and you leave it at that—as in this example, accepting the "yes"—when will you find out you have a "no?" Probably next Friday at noon. That may cause you a problem.

Developing a W⁴ (Who, What, When, Where, and How)

If the response is not a 100 percent "yes," it has some percentage of "no." You can accept this "no," or you can "up the level of control" to try to influence more "yes" by using the "no" strategies (see Figure 5-2 later in this chapter).

If you trust the person and he has come through before and you know he will come through—or, if the "yes" turning into a "no" (him not coming through) is no big deal to you—then accept the "yes." But there are other times when you need to get a commitment to a "yes," to pin down the commitment. An option is to push for what we call a who, what, when, where, and how (W⁴). Using our example, I would say, *"I really appreciate you agreeing, but I need to talk about this a little bit. I know that I'm being a little pushy, so I apologize."* Remember, whenever you up the level of control, you also increase the probability the other person will get defensive (**D↗T↘**). So you would only push for a W⁴ if you decide it is worth the risk.

Now, pushing for the who, what, when, where, and how, I'd say, *"This is really important to me. I need us to think through what it's really going to take to meet the Friday commitment. What I think really needs to happen is for you to look at your data bank and pull out the data, because I don't know what we have and I would like to know by Monday before you go home. Can you do that?"* Hopefully he would say *"yes."* Then I would say, *"Then, Tuesday morning I'll talk to you, and if there is any extra data or any holes in the data, you will have time to rectify these data issues. Then hopefully you could have the final report by Wednesday night?"* Again, hopefully he would say *"yes."* Now, what I've done is create some checkpoints or milestones so that, if I'm going to get a "no," I'll know it before next Friday. But I've also asked the person, before he walks away, to think it through.

Have you, when you've given an "easy yes" to someone, as soon as you left, had it turn into a "no?" You start to feel a little guilty and think, *"Why did I commit to that?"* Do you appreciate people sort of pushing you to pin it down before you walk away, if they do it respectfully? It really helps me. So, if you get a "yes," you may need to pin it down with a W^4.

Let me offer another classic example. Saturday morning, you ask your kids, *"Do you have any homework this weekend?"* What do they say? *"Sure."* *"Can you get it done without any help?"* *"Sure."*

How many of us have been in an argument Sunday night or Monday morning over this issue? The "easy yes" turns into a "no." Now what I suggest, and what parents have learned using this W^4 option: After getting the verbal "yes," you say, *"Okay, let's get your homework out and look at it, and make a plan."* Either they do, and you have a plan you can check, or they respond with their smoke screen, *"Oh, Dad, I'm going to the movie."* The "yes" turns to a "no." Now what are your options on Saturday morning? Walk away and accept it, or up the level of control. You've got to decide whether it's worth it. Do you want to invest the energy and take the risk of upping the level of control to deal with the issue Saturday morning, or do you want to deal with it Sunday night?

Dealing With "Nos" Effectively

Whenever you get a "no" from someone, to be effective you need to have options. Frequently we don't have effective options, especially if the "no" we are getting is emotional, because we react emotionally or defensively ourselves. This reaction is our own habit and is done without thinking ahead. When we react emotionally, we are not in control of the influencing process; our buttons have been pushed and, thus, there is a high probability that the interaction will lead to conflict. We are responding from our dinosaur brain and not our cortex.

It is normal to react in the face of conflict, but it is not very effective! Effective people have options!

The first step, then, is to recognize that you are getting a "no," irrespective of its verbal/emotional form. Don't react immediately from your dinosaur brain. (Silence helps this process.) Then, consider your options. Whenever you get a "no" from somebody, irrespective of the form, you have the options shown in Figure 5-2, starting at the bottom of the chart and, as the level of control inherent in each option increases, working up:

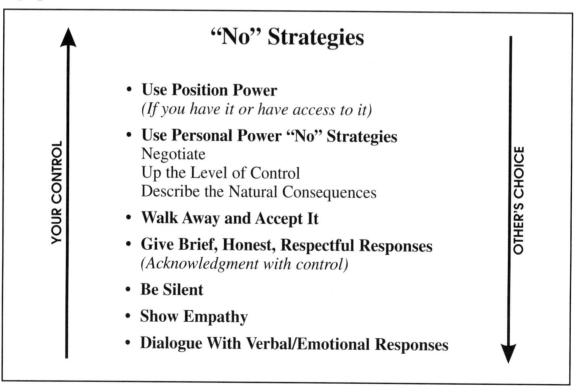

Figure 5-2

Dialogue

First of all, you *can* dialogue with the other person's smoke screen, and in fact that's what most people automatically do. Do you see the problem with this option, especially if the response you are getting is emotional? When you start dialoguing with the smoke screen, you get off the subject or you get your buttons pushed. Dialogue is fine if 1) you don't allow your buttons to get pushed, 2) the other person isn't too emotional, and/or 3) you can, while dialoguing, keep the conversation on the original issue.

Or you can skip the dialogue and use other options to go right to the "no" and start to work to change it to a "yes." Again, whenever you get a "no," and it has some verbal/emotional stuff around it, don't let the smoke get in your eyes.

Show Empathy

Showing empathy invites dialogue; it invites the other person to talk and to disclose her feelings and thoughts. It acknowledges her and shows understanding of her perspective.

If you can invite the other person to talk while not getting your buttons pushed or getting off your issue, then empathy is a very effective option. Delivering empathy then conveys sort of an implicit contract that the other person is invited to talk without being judged and that you will show understanding. Like all options, empathy has both a price—it may take time—and a probable payoff—defensiveness may go down and trust may go up (**D↘T↗**).

Be Silent

You do not have to immediately respond verbally to the other person's reaction. In fact, if you immediately respond, you are probably reacting from old habits and not using your cortex.

Silence is a very powerful option, especially when the other person is emotional. The use of silence with difficult emotional interactions is explored in detail in Chapter 8.

Give Brief, Honest, Respectful Responses

A very effective option is to acknowledge the other person with a brief, respectful response while also sticking with your issue and, thereby, keeping control of the process. This type of response is sort of halfway between inviting dialogue and being silent. These brief responses are not intended to avoid the issue and must be honest responses to the other person's statement.

Four brief responses that many people find useful are:

> *"That's not the issue."/"That's not the issue now."*

> *"Yes, that's true."*

> *"No, that's not true."*

> *"We will deal with that later."*

These responses are further described in Chapter 8.

Walk Away and Accept It

Now that you have received an emotional reaction, you may consider that investing more time and energy to try to change the person's "no" to a "yes" is not worth it. *Acceptance is an option!* If you choose this option you may:

1. Do the requested task yourself.
2. Get someone else to do it.
3. Walk away—let it go! Unless it is important and/or you cannot live with a "no."
4. Wait a short time—but not too long—and try again!

Walking away and accepting it is a viable life option and can and should be used at any time if upping the level of control is not worth it to you. Many of you have heard a condensed version of the original serenity prayer by Reinhold Niebuhr:

"God, grant me the serenity to accept the things I cannot change, courage to change the things I can, and wisdom to know the difference."

> **Acceptance truly means
> to let go of any future resentment about the same issue.**

Acceptance does not mean to avoid dealing with the issue directly while continuing to fester and carry anger or resentment.

Personal Power

Effective people get most of their influencing results through the use of their personal power. Remember the trust meter? Personal power is a positive reading on the trust meter. In this model, trust, credibility, influence, and personal power are synonymous. Personal power is earned. It is the power that has been ascribed to you by other people due to the way you have treated them. The higher your delivery of the Core Dimensions has been and the more (**D↘T↗**) type interactions you have had with these people, the more personal power you have with them. You have a different level of personal power with every person.

The Intensity of Feelings

In all your influencing it is very important to be aware of both your feelings and the feelings of the person you are trying to influence.

You need to be aware of your own feelings because the more emotional you are, the higher the probability that you may not be able to suspend your frame of reference and be objective, and the more vulnerable you are to reacting.

Imagine that all feelings, whether they be happy, strong, angry, scared, sad, weak, or confused, have an intensity that varies from low intensity to moderate intensity to high intensity. For anger, these different intensity feelings might be annoyed (low), angry (moderate), and furious (high). The higher the intensity of your feelings about a situation, the more preparation and practice you need before influencing or confronting so that you can operate at an intensity level within your control. This practice process is described in Chapter 9.

You also need to be aware of the intensity level of the feelings of the person you are influencing or confronting. This will enable you to choose an influencing option that will help you keep control of the influencing process and not let the emotional intensity lead to conflict. Typically, the higher the intensity of the other person's feelings, the less you will dialogue and the more you will up the level of control of the influencing process.

Responding with empathy to moderate- to high-intensity feeling levels is OK if you are highly skilled at delivering empathy, have the time and willingness to hear the emotional response, and can do so without allowing your buttons to be pushed. In most cases, if the other person's feelings are moderate- to high-intensity, it is best to use silence and the brief, honest, respectful responses described in Chapter 8.

Every time you interact, you influence (**D↗T↘** or **D↘T↗**). To the degree you have influenced in a way that the other person's defensiveness goes down and trust goes up, you have earned personal power.

Think of somebody who has mistreated you—talked behind your back, treated you unfavorably, not come through—and your trust of her is down. If she came to you today and asked you to do a favor, what are her chances of getting it? You see the problem? She lacks personal power with you.

All personal power means is that other people will give you a chance to influence them, that perhaps they will listen, try to understand, and perhaps consider what you are asking them to do. They may still disagree and say "no." Personal power is no guarantee. It just gives you a chance.

Imagine going to a person and using a reasonable level of assertiveness, asking him to do something. He thinks about it and says, *"Given my priorities and what I think I need to be spending my time and energy on right now, I don't think I ought to be doing that."* You're getting a "no" at the moment. At that point, you decide either to accept it or to up the level of control. If you up the level of control, you would hopefully move to the use of your personal power. Using personal power, in essence, is an appeal or a "please" to the person.

As I have worked with effective people over the years, it has become apparent to me that there are three most frequently used personal power strategies, as illustrated in Figure 5-3, working from the bottom up:

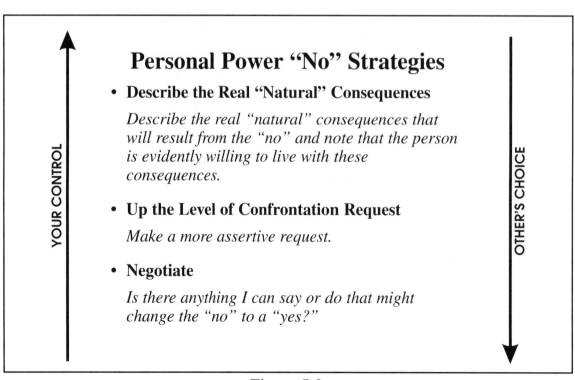

Figure 5-3

There are other strategies, but our focus is on these three and, even more so in this book, on the *confrontation* option. These personal power strategies require that you not react, but engage the cortex first.

Negotiate

I firmly believe that all disagreements could and should be handled most effectively by using negotiation. I hope all of your confrontations lead to negotiation and not to conflict!

Most people have this negotiation skill in their repertoire, and yet don't use it as effectively, or as often as possible, because they get their buttons pushed and react.

Negotiation requires that two people come together, face to face, to resolve an issue on which they do not agree. It requires that they both:

1. State what they want.

2. Understand the other person's request.

3. Work toward a resolution that can leave both people satisfied.

This option then, invites the person who is giving you a "no" at the moment to help you find a way to get to a "yes."

There are many verbal ways to request negotiation, so you should find a format that is comfortable to you.

Examples of negotiation:

"Is there anything I could say or do?"

"What do we need to do to make this happen?" "Can you help me find another option?"

"Are you willing to negotiate?"

"Is there anything I can do for you that, if I do that, you will do this for me?"

"Who else can help me?"

All of these options are saying, *"I acknowledge the 'no.' What do we need to do to get to a 'yes'?"*

Frequently, when getting a "no," we react by saying "Why?" or "Why not?" When you react with either of these questions instead of asking a negotiation question, you create a high probability of losing control of the process.

What's wrong with asking *"Why?"* or *"Why not?"* when you get a "no?" It's that you are saying, *"Give me all the reasons in the world why you can't do that."* And you know what the person will do? They'll tell you what's wrong with the equipment, what's wrong with the people, what's wrong with you, how you screwed up in the past, what's wrong with management and the organization and everything else. When you're all done, what are you still sitting there with? A "no!"—Poor investment! Poor option! Asking *"Why?"* to a "no" is inviting a smoke screen!

Remember, the goal of influencing is to move toward a "yes." When you ask *"Why?"* you're saying, *"Embellish the 'no'."* Once you get this embellishment, you say, *"Gee whiz, you're right,"* and you probably retract your request, get defensive, or start discussing one of the other person's issues.

Up the Level of Confrontation Request
The Progressive Confrontation Model to be presented in Chapter 6 allows you options to gradually up your level of control of the influencing process depending upon the degree of control/choice that you deem appropriate.

The confrontation options, in order of increasing level of control communicated, are the Discrepancy Confrontation (low control/high choice), the Behavior Request Confrontation (moderate control/choice), and the Accountability Confrontation (high control/low choice).

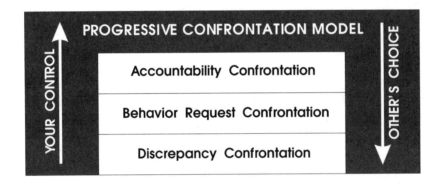

Figure 5-4

This option of upping the level of confrontation request involves making your initial request using a reasonable degree of control/choice. If this level of confrontation does not work, you're getting a "no," and you will have the option of using another confrontation format to up your level of control.

Describe the "Natural" Consequences
A lot of times people give you a "no" without thinking about what's going to happen. They react, automatically, without their cortex engaged—their buttons were pushed! If they thought about the consequences that would occur by giving a "no," they probably would not have said "no." Also, if their "no" is emotional, they are probably not

even aware that they are giving a "no." This option involves telling them the consequences of their "no." It's done with a calm, rational voice, and basically states, *"Look, you're giving a 'no,' and you have a right to, but by giving this 'no,' the consequences down the line are going to be such."*

There is a difference between threatening with consequences that are fabricated and describing what are called natural consequences, a term believed to be first used by Rudolf Dreikurs.

A natural consequence is something that naturally occurs. It is the natural outcome of the cause-effect progression in life. It will naturally occur, with you in or out of the equation.

Examples of Consequences		
Behavior	**Natural Consequences**	**Unnatural (Fabricated) Consequences**
"If you don't do what you promised...	*people won't trust your word in the future."*	*I'll report you and make you look bad."*
"If you don't do your homework...	*you'll be unprepared, feel badly, and probably get a poorer grade."*	*I'll take the TV away."*

Figure 5-5

This option describes for the person the real consequences of his behavior without judgment or malice. It is stated matter-of-factly. Often this dose of objective reality will change a "no" to a "yes." If it doesn't, you're getting another "no" and can choose from amongst your options.

In summary, the three Personal Power "No" Strategies are:

1. Negotiate.
2. Up the level of confrontation request.
3. Describe the real "natural" consequences.

Position Power

Let's review. You make your request and start the influencing process. If you get a "yes," you're on your way. But if you get a "no"—and remember that "nos" could come in any format—you have two generic options. Walk away and accept it, because it's not worth upping the level of control, or up your level of control to try to change the "no" to "yes." If you decide to up your level of control, notice that the next level (see

Figure 5-2) that you preferably use is your personal power. If the personal power options do not work or if you choose to up your level of control to a very high level, you could use *position power*.

Position power is the power to give and take away rewards and punishments. You have this power by virtue of your title—supervisor, lead, manager, director, and, for a while, parent. Most of you who are not supervisors do not have position power, although you do have access to position power through the chain of command. This book is about learning to influence people without position power, because you don't want to use it anyway unless absolutely necessary.

What happens when you use position power? Basically you are saying, *"Look, if you don't do it, you'll be punished."* What happens when you use that level of control? Defensiveness often goes up and trust goes down (**D⬀T⬊**). So it is best not to use position power unless you have to, and then, only if you are willing to pay the price. If you're going to ground your kids, that's position power. You had better be willing to pay the price, and the reason for doing it had better be that important.

To summarize what you have learned:

- Tell people what you want and be specific.
- Deliver a high level of the Core Dimensions. Most of us think we do, but may not because of old habits.
- Perceive if you're getting a "yes" or "no." Anything less than a "yes" is a "no" at the moment. Neither one is bad.
- If you get a "yes," you may need to pin it down with a W^4.
- If you get a "no," your two options are to walk away and accept it or up the level of control.
- If you up the level of control, use personal power. Negotiate, up the level of confrontation, or describe the natural consequences.
- If you still have a "no," consider using (if you have it or have access to it) position power.

When you want to address a risky or emotional issue with another person or you have tried to address an issue and are getting a "no," you need the skill to up your level of control of the influencing process. The progressive confrontation options presented in the next chapter may be helpful.

CHAPTER 6

The Progressive Confrontation Model

Confrontation is a process! You have options about when and where to confront, what level of confrontation to use, and, as you experience the other person's reactions, how to respond in terms of upping your level of control of the influencing process.

> **The confrontation only starts the process . . .**
> **you then need to keep control of the process**
> **so that it does not become hurtful.**

The progressive confrontation options are called "progressive" because they allow you several alternatives to progressively increase or decrease your level of control/choice as you choose. Remember, each option, based on the level of control/choice conveyed, has an investment of time, energy, and risk, and a price (consequences). You choose how to fit the process into your value system, comfort zone, and relationships. The Progressive Confrontation Model is consistent with the original influencing process described in Chapter 2.

Remember the three parts to effective confrontation and influencing:

1. tell the person specifically what you want in a way that lessens defensiveness and increases trust (**D↘T↗**);

2. perceive the person's response, whether you're getting a "yes" or a "no"; and

3. respond to the other person's reaction in a way that keeps the interaction on the issue (yours), respectful and rational, and moving toward a clear "yes" or "no" without a fight.

The three progressive confrontation request options are the **Discrepancy Confrontation** (low control/high choice), the **Behavior Request Confrontation** (moderate control/moderate choice), and the **Accountability Confrontation** (high control/low choice).

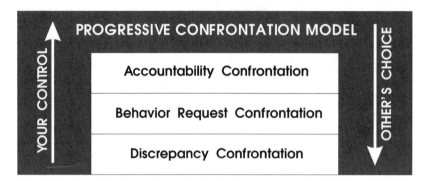

Figure 6-1

Each format has its special use. A great majority of the time you will be able to resolve the issue using only the format with which you initiated your confrontation. Occasionally you may use more than one format during a confrontation, depending on whether you choose to increase or decrease your level of control at the time. The three formats vary according to the inherent level of control and choice communicated to the other person. The three confrontation options are described in full detail in Figure 6-2 and Figure 6-3.

Figure 6-2 describes the characteristics of each format, along with an example. Figure 6-3 presents the actual components of each format.

Notice the arrows on the right and left sides of Figure 6-2 and Figure 6-3. As you go up the chart, you increase your level of control (up the level of control). As you go down the chart, you lower your level of control and convey that the other person has more choice.

Progressive Confrontation Options

Accountability Confrontation
(High Control/Low Choice)

- Allows no dialogue
- Influences accountability
- Makes the issue either "yes" or "no"
- Gets at the issue of willingness

"I need to know if you are willing to be more respectful of me by talking to me in a calm voice, listening to my point of view, and, if you disagree, saying so instead of putting me down—'yes' or 'no'?"

Behavior Request Confrontation
(Moderate to High Control/Moderate Choice)

- Very direct request
- Gets to the issue immediately
- Basic building block of the Progressive Confrontation Model
- Most frequently used confrontation format

"I would like you to be more respectful of me when we disagree. For example, talk to me in a calm voice, saying 'I disagree' instead of putting me down. As a result, I'll feel that you care and I won't have a tendency to withdraw."

Discrepancy Confrontation
(Low Control/High Choice)

- Indirect
- Invites dialogue
- Requests that the other person be "open"
- Lowest risk

"I'm confused because on the one hand you want us to have a mutually respectful relationship, while on the other hand, when we have a disagreement, I get judged and put down."

YOUR CONTROL

OTHER'S CHOICE

Figure 6-2

Progressive Confrontation Formats

YOUR CONTROL (left vertical arrow, pointing up)

OTHER'S CHOICE (right vertical arrow, pointing down)

Accountability Confrontation

"I need to know if you are willing to (1) (specific desirable behavior that you are requesting), "yes" or "no?"

No matter what the response, translate it into a "yes" or a "no" until the person becomes accountable. Use your "yes" or "no" strategies.

Behavior Request Confrontation

"I (1) (degree of control/choice word or phrase) (2) (specific desirable behavior you are requesting) and, as a result (3) (consequences)."

Degree of Control/Choice Words	*Consequences*
Demand (*rarely used*)	Negative consequences to you, him, others, the team, or the relationship
Expect	
Need	or
Want	
Prefer	Positive consequences to you, him, others, the team, or the relationship
Would like you to	
Would like you to consider	

Discrepancy Confrontation

"I'm (1) (your feeling), because on the one hand (2) (positive attribute of the person), while on the other hand, (3) (the undesirable behavior that is discrepant with the positive attribute)."

Point out, without judgment, the discrepancy in the other person's behavior, i.e., between what they've said, done, felt, thought, needed, promised, envisioned, or believed. You need to be willing to listen to the other person and respond (empathy recommended).

Figure 6-3

Before you begin to learn how to deliver each of these three progressive confrontation options, let's quickly review what you have already learned about confrontation.

Remember, confrontation is a request for behavior change. To confront means to go to another person and tell her specifically what you want in a way that lessens defensiveness. You're not devaluing, creating conflict, or harming the person. You're making a respectful request and she has a right to say "yes" or "no."

Typically we avoid confrontation because the only option we have learned creates conflict by telling the person what she has done wrong in an emotional and/or judgmental way. To be effective when someone else's behavior causes you a problem, you immediately decide to either confront the issue or to walk away, accept it, and let it go. If you decide to confront it, then only wait long enough to:

- calm down;
- prepare an effective confrontation; and
- choose the time and place.

If you decide to accept it, work on letting it go and getting rid of any resentment.

If you are presently ineffective at confrontation, it is because you either 1) don't confront, don't let it go, then continue to fester, or 2) confront in a way that creates defensiveness.

As a way of learning these skills, I suggest that you work through and develop a real confrontation. Please use the confrontation practice worksheet provided in each section in this chapter. A complete worksheet is provided at the end of Chapter 7. Additional copies of the worksheets are in Appendix B.

Behavior Request Confrontation

Effective people request what they want from others. They are not vague or unclear, nor are they hurtful or devaluing. They see influencing as being quite simple. They start with requesting what they want. This is sort of "putting a stake in the ground"— it starts the process, like serving a tennis ball to begin a point.

The basic building block of the Progressive Confrontation Model is called a *Behavior Request Confrontation*. It is in the middle of Figures 6-1, 6-2, 6-3, and 6-4 because it offers moderate-control/moderate-choice options.

The Behavior Request Confrontation format evolved as a way to eliminate any ingredient that would trigger defensiveness:

- Stating the *"I" message* eliminates the *"blaming you."*
- Stating the *desired behavior* eliminates the focus on the *undesirable behavior.*
- Stating the *positive consequences* eliminates the threat of *negative consequences.*

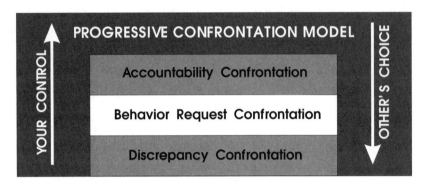

Figure 6-4

Advantages

As I have worked with people over the years helping them prepare, practice, and deliver confrontations, a great majority of confrontations have been delivered using this format.

The Behavior Request Confrontation is the key to the entire Progressive Confrontation Model for several reasons:

1. It demands that you be clear and specific about what you want.
2. It is a natural way of talking, so it comes easily.
3. If used frequently, it can be preventive in nature. If you let people know what you want, there is less chance that they will do things that are undesirable to you.
4. If you get "lost" during a confrontation, i.e., lose your train of thought, get flustered, or become reactive, you can always restate your Behavior Request Confrontation like a "broken record." It will be your life raft when in trouble.
5. If you choose to deliver your confrontation using the Discrepancy Confrontation format (described in the next section) and you get a "no," the next option, if you choose to up your level of control and not walk away, will be to use the Behavior Request Confrontation.

If people do not know what you want, they will probably not meet your expectations and, therefore, you have a potential conflict. If you tell them what you want, they will often do it and, thus, you have *prevented* potential conflict.

> ***"If you don't know where you are going,***
> ***you'll probably end up somewhere else."***
>
> —L. J. Peter
> *The Peter Principle*

Components

The format for the Behavior Request Confrontation has three components:

> *"I <u>(1) (degree of control/choice word or phrase)</u> <u>(2) (specific</u> <u>desirable behavior you are requesting)</u> and, as a result, <u>(3) (positive consequences)</u>."*

> **Example:** *"I need you to be more supportive of me as we work together; by that I mean, when you finish work at the end of the day, check with me to see if I need help, and when I ask for help, respond pleasantly and with respect to either help me or help me find an option. As a result, I will be more productive, less stressed, and more willing to help you."*

"I" Messages

It is important that you are comfortable using "I" messages to express yourself, and especially so when confronting. It ensures that the request is yours and that you have owned or personalized it. It also increases the probability that the other person's response will start with an "I" (there is no guarantee!). The "I" implies clear accountability—yours and theirs— thus, no "beating around the issue." Without an "I" message, the request often slips into a "blaming you," which increases the probability of (D↗T↘).

Degree of Control/Choice Word or Phrase

As you have learned, this phrase communicates your level of urgency, the issue's importance to you, and your assertiveness and control. You state the "I" message using the *degree of control/choice word or phrase* that is appropriate to the issue, situation, and your comfort level. Keep in mind that you can change the level of control as you proceed with the confrontation, although you will be more effective if you think this out before you deliver your confrontation. In Figure 6-5 is a partial list of frequently used degree of control/choice words in approximate order of increasing control:

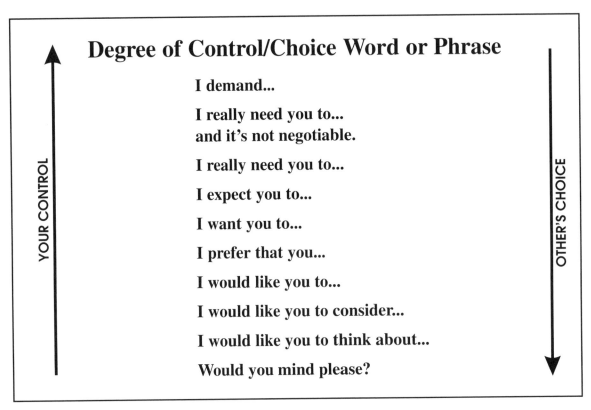

Figure 6-5

None of these words are right or wrong. Each conveys a level of importance that will elicit some predictable level of reaction in terms of the other person's defensiveness and trust.

The key is to communicate the level of importance that you really mean.

Remember, the higher the level of control communicated, the higher the risk of defensiveness going up and trust going down. Imagine, tonight, at home, requesting of someone:

"I would like you to think about helping me with the housework."

In terms of the importance of your request, what does the person hear? It's not really important! He also hears that it's OK if he doesn't do it!

This request is very polite, and being polite and "non-pushy" is great *if it works!* But you could also be very assertive (convey a high level of importance and control) while also being respectful.

Don't confuse assertiveness and politeness . . . they are not mutually exclusive! Consider another way of making the request:

"I really need you to help me with the housework tonight."

If delivered with a firm yet soft voice and open, relaxed body language, it would be polite, but would also convey an entirely different level of importance.

Does this second request sound more important and urgent than the first? . . . Yes! Is it OK if the person does not do it? . . . Not quite as OK!

Most people are very comfortable giving and receiving requests using:

"I would like you to _____ ."

"I want you to _____ ."

"I need you to _____ ."

In all cases, choose the degree of control/choice word that on the one hand conveys your intended importance, while also lessening the other person's defensiveness.

It is very important that you have a very high degree of control/choice word or phrase that you feel comfortable using when you want to "draw the line" or establish a strong, non-negotiable boundary on an important issue. I am not comfortable with *"I demand"* so instead, use *"I really need you to (request) and it's not negotiable."*

Gender Differences

There seem to be some gender differences in terms of what degree of control/ choice words are comfortable, acceptable, and most frequently used.

Many women report that they, without being aware of it, have learned to use degree of control/choice words that are lower on control and higher on choice, such as:

"Would you _____?"

"I would like you to consider _____."

"How about doing _____?"

These requests are fine, but do not convey a very high level of importance, so may be misperceived.

As I have worked with women who have become aware of these verbal habits and who want to have more options to be assertive, they discover that often when they use the above phrases, they really mean more genuinely:

"I would like you to _____."

"I want you to _____."

"I really need you to _____."

Many women feel that they have been taught to be deferent, soothers, and pacifiers and, thus, have developed a low level of control/high-choice vocabulary. They want to retain that part of themselves, but may also want to have options to be more assertive (indicate a higher level of control).

Men, on the other hand, often report that they have been taught and, therefore, feel more comfortable using a higher level of control/low-choice vocabulary. They too report that they are not always aware of the control/choice words they use by habit.

Examples of some of these higher-control/lower-choice words are:

"I expect you to _____."

"I assume you'll _____."

These higher-control type requests are also fine, but result in their being perceived as too controlling, dominant, and insensitive, when, in fact, that may not be their intent.

So, men and women alike need to be aware of their control/choice words and choose the word that matches their inside intentions.

Specific Desirable Behavior

The key to the entire confrontation process is being specific about what you want. If you are not specific, either of the following responses may happen:

1. People will give a "yes" to your vague request. They can then do whatever they want. They get to interpret the specifics—what you meant.

2. People will begin to argue with you about *what you mean* during the confrontation and the probability is high that you will get defensive or off the original issue—your worst fear!

Let me give you a couple of examples in Figure 6-6. Notice the difference:

Being Specific	
Non-Specific	**Specific**
"I would like you to be more respectful of me."	*"I would like you to be more respectful of me when we disagree; for example, talk to me in a calm voice, saying 'I disagree' instead of putting me down. As a result, I'll feel that you care and I won't have a tendency to withdraw."*
"You didn't do the dishes this morning."	*"I really need you to do the dishes as agreed; by that I mean immediately upon finishing eating, rinse the food off and place each dish and utensil in the right spot in the dishwasher, rinse the food down the drain so the sink looks clean, and start the dishwasher. If you do, I'll feel that you are doing your fair share and won't want to hassle you in the evening."*

Figure 6-6

As you have already discovered, being specific seems to be a skill that most people, irrespective of education, background, or position, have not developed to a sufficient degree. So, don't feel inadequate if you struggle with being specific! This is your chance to learn.

I have found that people who are able to be specific use a logical, mental, step-by-step process:

1. They think of the undesirable behavior that's bothering them.

    "He sure is disrespectful . . ."

2. They change the undesirable behavior to the desirable behavior—the opposite.

    "I'd like him to be respectful . . ."

3. They add specificity (if the desirable behavior is general, then add specificity). Give two or three examples of what he could say or do that would behaviorally define the more general term in your request.

    "I need you to be respectful;

    by that I mean *(give two to three examples of what he would say or do),"*

    or, **for example** *(give two to three examples of what he would say or do),"*

    or, **as demonstrated by** *(give two to three examples of what he would say or do),"*

    and as a result, if you do (positive consequences)."

    Example: *"I need you to be more respectful; by that I mean when you talk to me I would like you to smile and be pleasant; when I ask for help I would like you to help me and not tell others I'm incompetent; when I talk I would like you to listen and not interrupt; and, as a result, I'll feel supported, I'll be more productive, and I'll want to invest more in our relationship."*

Consequences

Often people do not do what you want them to do just because you want them to! Most people behave the way they do because by behaving this way they either get the positive consequences they want, or avoid the negative consequences they don't want.

So, the last component of an effective Behavior Request Confrontation is to tell the person the consequences that, from your point of view, will result if he changes and does the requested behavior. These consequences can either be described as the positive consequences if he does or the negative consequences if he doesn't.

To decrease the probability of defensiveness increasing and trust decreasing (**D⬈T⬊**), it is best, if possible, to describe the positive consequences to you, him, the relationship, others, trust, feelings, or productivity.

Examples of consequences:

> *". . . and as a result:*
>
> *you will be seen as more supportive."*
>
> *our relationship will be better."*
>
> *she will be able to pass algebra."*
>
> *my trust of you will increase."*
>
> *I will be more productive."*

By describing positive consequences, you have remained positive and non-threatening. People often understand, and this approach works.

At other times, people do not respond to positive consequences. I am continually surprised that some people respond in life only to avoid negative consequences. Try as you may to describe the positive consequences, these people are not influenced. So, a necessary option is to be able and willing to tell such people what negative consequences will occur if they do not change their behavior. You may not be comfortable with this option because it feels like a threat. If you describe the negative *natural consequences,* you are not fabricating consequences and, therefore, may not feel quite so guilty. In fact, these natural consequences are what *will* occur if you don't confront and the person continues the undesired behavior.

Often, you even need to qualify that these natural consequences may occur from *your experience*. These consequences are usually not something you are going to make happen . . . they will happen as a normal, predictable event in life's natural progression, from your point of view. Often, the natural consequence is to the relationship, trust, or your feelings.

Examples of natural consequences:

> *". . . and as a result, if you don't,*
>
> *. . . my trust for you will decrease."*
>
> *. . . she may not pass algebra."*
>
> *. . . our relationship will deteriorate."*
>
> *. . . you will be viewed as not supportive."*
>
> *. . . I will be less productive."*

In many confrontations, people initiate their Behavior Request Confrontation describing the positive consequences that will result if the person will change. If describing these consequences does not get a "yes," they up the level of control during the same confrontation by giving the same Behavior Request Confrontation, but then describing the negative consequences that will occur if the person does not comply. Making this transition from positive to negative consequences occurs frequently and naturally. As you prepare for your confrontation, you need both types of consequences in mind.

Practice

As a way of integrating these skills, I suggest you develop a Behavior Request Confrontation using the steps described on the worksheet (see Figure 6-7). Think of someone in your life whose behavior is causing you a problem, and as a consequence you feel distress, resentment, frustration, or hurt and want to consider asking them to change.

Behavior Request Confrontation Worksheet

1. Describe the person's undesirable behavior (what she/he is doing that is causing you a problem).

   _____

   _____

   _____

2. What do you want the person to do? (the opposite of what you don't like)

   I would like him/her to: _____

   _____

   _____

   _____

3. Add specificity (if what you are requesting is described with a non-specific term, add specificity).

   I would like you to _____

   _____

   by that I mean _____

   _____

   or, for example _____

   _____

   or, as demonstrated by _____

   _____

   or, more specifically _____

   _____

4. Add the positive consequences if she/he changes.

   . . . and, as a result, if you do, _____

   _____

   _____

   _____

Figure 6-7

Discrepancy Confrontation

There are times when, instead of being direct about what you want and, thus, forcing the issue, you may want to approach the issue in a softer, lower-risk way. If so, the option to use is the *Discrepancy Confrontation*.

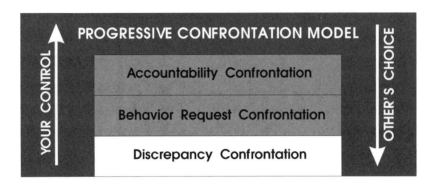

Figure 6-8

There are specific advantages and disadvantages to using the Discrepancy Confrontation, especially to initiate the confrontation.

Advantages

- It is lower-risk (lower control/higher choice than the Behavior Request Confrontation).
- It allows the other person to "own" the issues and identify the problem.
- It invites the other person to engage in a dialogue and to tell his or her side of the story or issue.

The Discrepancy Confrontation should be used under the following conditions:

- The other person is someone who you perceive would want to resolve the issue, who you want to invite into dialogue and discussion, and who will most likely respond from his cortex and not his dinosaur brain.
- The other person is aware enough to be able to perceive a discrepancy and is not so emotional that he may not perceive objectively and rationally.
- You want to initiate a conversation about an issue with low risk on your part.
- You are not sure the person did the undesirable behavior and you want to hear his side of the story.
- You want to make a second or follow-up confrontation. Specifically, you already confronted at a Behavior Request Confrontation level and got a verbal "yes," but the person isn't doing what he agreed—you are getting a behavioral "no."

Disadvantages

- It does not directly or clearly define what you want.

- Because it invites dialogue, it gives more freedom for an emotional outburst, or for other issues to be referenced.

Typically, a Discrepancy Confrontation is not an effective option if:

- The other person will be emotionally volatile and/or out of control, such as angry, defensive, or belligerent.

- You wish to get directly to the issue, i.e., your requested change of behavior.

Discrepancy Confrontation as a "Helping" Strategy

The Discrepancy Confrontation evolved from the helping professions. Its goal was to help clients explore, understand, own (personalize), and resolve discrepant issues in their behavior. (Berenson, B.G. and Mitchell, K.M.)

It was intended to be used only when the confronter, in this case the helper, was highly trained in the use of facilitative empathy. Since the Discrepancy Confrontation invites dialogue and exploration, it is very important that you consider responding with empathy.

This Progressive Confrontation Model expands the use of the Discrepancy Confrontation format to other than just a "helping" relationship. It is an even more effective option if you are skilled at empathy. *The Art of Helping* by Robert R. Carkhuff is an excellent resource in learning the skill of empathy.

Components

The format for the Discrepancy Confrontation has three components:

"I'm (1) (your feeling) because on the one hand (2) (describe some real, positive attribute of the person, something he has said, done, promised, needed, dreamed of, thought, or believed), while on the other hand, (3) (describe the undesirable behavior that is discrepant or contradicts the positive part of him that you described)."

Example: *"I'm confused, because on the one hand you perceive yourself as a supportive and cooperative person, while on the other hand, the last three days I have been really busy and when you finished work, I was not offered any help."*

Your Feeling

Share your true, genuine feeling and do not pull punches. The other person probably senses your true feelings anyway, so be straight!

> *"I feel disappointed."/"I'm disappointed."*

> *"I feel confused."/"I'm confused."*

> *"I feel hurt."/"I'm hurt."*

> *"I feel angry."/"I'm angry."*

Positive Attribute of the Other Person

When you think about the undesirable behavior that is causing you the problem, with what part or attribute of this person is this undesirable behavior inconsistent? Often this positive attribute is something the person perceives, believes, wants, needs, has said, has promised, or has done before.

She *perceives* herself to be cooperative, but is not very approachable. He *wants* to be valued and liked, but talks behind other people's backs. She *needs* your cooperation, but frequently gives excuses when asked to help. He *has said* he is committed to a course of action, but is not meeting the agreed-upon deadlines. She has *promised* to do the dishes, but always has to be reminded. He *has been* honest before, but recently seems to be withholding important information.

The Discrepant Behavior

Describe the undesirable behavior that is causing you a problem. This is the easy part, because you have already articulated this behavior as you developed your Behavior Request Confrontation.

Two cautions: As you describe the undesirable behavior, it is very natural for either of the following to slip into your statement:

> 1. "blaming you"
> 2. judgmental terms

Do your best to eliminate both by modifying the wording. You may want to refer back to the Discrepancy Confrontation example. Notice how easily the "blaming you" could have slipped into the following example:

> *". . . while on the other hand, the last three days, when I have been really busy and when **you** finished work, **you** did not offer to help."*

When this blaming and judgmentalness is included, the probability increases that the other person might become defensive. There are times when you cannot eliminate the "blaming you" without losing the entire impact and focus of the confrontation. If you do leave it in, be aware that it will probably "tweak" defensiveness, be prepared to risk getting that consequence, and be ready to deal with the emotional reaction without losing control of the process.

Practice

Now, using the Discrepancy Confrontation Worksheet (Figure 6-9), write a Discrepancy Confrontation using the same issue you used to write your Behavior Request Confrontation (see Figure 6-7).

Discrepancy Confrontation Worksheet

Using the same issue you used when you wrote your Behavior Request Confrontation, write a Discrepancy Confrontation:

I feel _____ because on the one hand
    (1) (your feeling)

_____ ,
    (2) (positive attribute of the person)

while on the other hand, _____

_____ ,
    (3) (undesirable behavior)

_____ .

Figure 6-9

Accountability Confrontation

Have you ever been in a discussion about an issue when the conversation seemed to go "on and on" and "round and round"? You seemed to be getting nowhere, like you were chasing your tail. Did you have trouble trying to bring that kind of interaction to a head?

This often happens in confrontation. You have confronted (made your request) and the other person continues to bring up other issues. You restate your request and other issues are brought in. At some point you need an option to "force the issue" to closure, if you choose to risk doing so.

A very effective option for bringing an interaction to "a head" is what I call the *Accountability Confrontation*. As with other influencing options, using this confrontation format has its advantages and disadvantages.

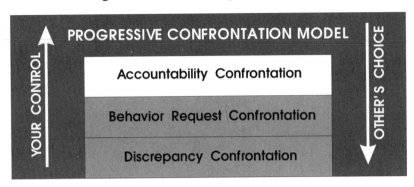

Figure 6-10

Advantages

- It gives you a high level of control of the influencing process.
- It switches the focus from the issue you are requesting to the other person's willingness or unwillingness to commit to a "yes."
- It forces you to be absolutely honest regarding the consequences that will follow if you get a "no."

So, if you choose this format, you should have decided that:

- You want to force a clear "yes" or "no."
- You are finished with dialogue.
- You are ready, if you get a "no," to tell the person the consequences of her "no" and to follow up with some action.

Disadvantages

- Using this confrontation format will bring the issue to a head. If you are not willing to hear a "no," do not use this format.
- The person may feel that she is being strongly influenced to be accountable and may react defensively.

Components

This format is very simple! Literally, use the identical wording from the Behavior Request Confrontation, except to drop the consequences from that confrontation format, and substitute the words "yes?" or "no?".

> *"I (1) (degree of control/choice word) to know if you are willing to (2) (specific behavior from Behavior Request Confrontation format), 'yes' or 'no'?"*

> *or*

> *"I (1) (degree of control/choice word) to know if you are willing to make a commitment to me, right now, to (2) (specific behavior from Behavior Request Confrontation format), 'yes' or 'no'?"*

The second format requests a different kind of commitment than the first: a personal commitment to the requester, rather than a commitment to do something. It is perceived as very powerful and very assertive.

> **Example:** *"I need to know if you are willing from now on, when you finish work, to come to me and ask if I need any help, 'yes' or 'no'?"*

Degree of Control/Choice Word or Phrase

Choose the degree of control/choice word that articulates your urgency and the importance of the issue. Since this is a strong, "bring-the-issue-to-a-head" confrontation, do not understate the importance to you. Usually an appropriate degree of control/choice word is at least at the *"I need"* level. Refer to Figure 6-5 for other degree of control/choice words.

Specific Behavior

This behavior is exactly the behavior you developed in your Behavior Request Confrontation format. Use that behavior, with its total specificity.

If you choose to use or progress to the Accountability Confrontation level, you should have decided that you will no longer dialogue. The power of this option is forcing the issue into either a "yes" or "no."

If you get a "yes," proceed to get a commitment using the W^4 (who, what, when, where, and how) option.

If you get anything less than a "yes," you are getting a "no" at the moment, so you either walk away and accept it or up the level of control. Your only remaining options are to negotiate or to tell the person the consequences of the "no." (You cannot up the level of confrontation because you are already at the highest level.)

If you get a clear "no," i.e., the person says, *"No, I can't"* or *"No, I won't,"* then ask, *"Is there anything I can say or do to get you to change your mind?"* (negotiation). If you still get a "no," then describe the consequences of the "no" (natural consequences), and if you still do not get a change to a "yes," end this interaction.

If you get a smoke-screen "no," i.e., any verbal/emotional response less than a clear "yes," interpret it as a "no" by saying, *"I take your response as a 'no'."* Proceed as outlined in the paragraph above. Do not get drawn back into a dialogue!

Practice

Now write an Accountability Confrontation using the Accountability Confrontation Worksheet (Figure 6-11), using the same issue you used in your Behavior Request Confrontation and Discrepancy Confrontation

---

Accountability Confrontation Worksheet

Write an Accountability Confrontation using the same issue you used in Figure 6-7 and Figure 6-9:

"I _____

          (1) (degree of control/choice word)

to know if you are willing to _____

_____

          (2) (specific behavior)

_____ *'yes' or 'no'?"*

Figure 6-11

This Progressive Confrontation Model allows you to choose a confrontation level based on urgency, trust, level of control, past experience, and risk.

It also provides, if you get a "no," options to up the level of control incrementally so that you are not forced to either fold (flight) or use force (fight).

As you incrementally up the level of control, you have points at which you either walk away or choose another option. Ultimately the question becomes, how many different "nos" are you going to get before you see that you have a real *"no!"*?

Now that you know how to deliver the confrontation, the next step is to be prepared to deal with the other person's reaction so that you can keep control of the influencing process.

CHAPTER 7

Preparing for the Confrontation

There are a number of confrontations or requests for change that you will deliver where there is very little risk. You will make those confrontations using either the Discrepancy Confrontation or the Behavior Request Confrontation format. The other person will not be defensive and you will easily resolve the issue. In fact, if you use these skills frequently (early and quickly) to deal with issues, you will often avoid the tough confrontations.

But from time to time in life, there will be situations where you feel significant emotion, risk, and vulnerability. In these cases, it is imperative that you develop a strategy so that you can keep control of the process and prevent conflict.

The sole purpose of the strategy outlined in this chapter is to prepare you to use your cortex and to not have to react or "think on your feet" during the confrontation, because you will be under emotional duress.

Thus, the key to being effective at tough confrontations is to prepare, prepare, prepare . . . to keep control of the influencing process because you are emotional, there is perceived risk, or the other person may be emotional.

The natural tendency in these emotional situations is to be reactive and to allow your buttons to be pushed. If you do, without meaning to, you may tell the person what he has done wrong (the undesirable behavior), become emotionally reactive—angry or defensive—get off the issue, and/or become judgmental. Any of these reactions will result in the other person becoming reactive, emotional, and defensive (**D↗T↘**). The more emotional and risky the issue, the more you should prepare!

Preparing for a confrontation is a preventive process. It is a matter of thinking and emotionalizing through all of the possible pitfalls or things that may go wrong so that, if any of them occur, you will be ready to keep the confrontation:

1. on *your* issue;

2. on *one* issue;

3. calm and respectful; and

4. moving toward a clear "yes" or "no."

Preparation engages your cortex and can prevent your buttons from getting pushed. Remember the Dinosaur Brain Analogy in Chapter 4.

There are two steps to preparation:

1. Develop a strategy for delivering the confrontation using the steps described in this chapter.

2. Practice dealing with emotional reactions (smoke screens), as outlined in Chapter 9.

The Strategy for the Confrontation

If possible, any time there is risk, emotion, or vulnerability involved in an influencing situation, take time to think through the following strategy questions. These steps are offered as suggested guidelines to prepare for the confrontation:

1. Decide what, specifically, you want from the person.

2. Determine if the return for delivering this confrontation is worth the investmentof time, energy, and risk.

3. Determine what is the WPPSS (worst possible, possible scary scenario).

4. Determine what you are going to do if you get a "no."

5. Determine what progressive confrontation level you should use to initiate the confrontation. Consider past investment, urgency, and risk.

6. Have specific facts or examples of the undesirable behavior ready, if necessary.

7. Consider what "no" behavior you expect.

8. Decide how you plan to respond to this "no" behavior.

9. Decide how much time you plan to spend with this "no" behavior.

10. Determine what your next confrontation or "no" strategy will be if you get a "no" on your first attempt.

11. Determine if it would help to put your confrontation in context.

12. Decide if you are confronting the right person first and if you have your "ducks" in line?

Shepherding Analogy

This analogy has a flaw: people are not sheep! I do not mean to imply that they are!

But imagine herding a group of sheep. Since sheep are frequently herded from behind, the path in front of them needs to be clear, with no escapes. So, before herding, the herder goes up the lane and opens the gate to the corral or pasture where the herd is to be driven.

In relation to this Progressive Confrontation Model, this target is our "yes" and represents a clear, specific written behavior request.

The herder then backtracks along the lane, closing off all other possible escapes. He closes gates and checks to make sure all fence posts are solid, wire is taut, and boards are nailed tight. Sheep will test all possible escapes and if they find a loose post or board, they will push and break through. They will find a weak spot or a vulnerability.

Once the route is clear and readied, the herding begins. The sheepdog starts the herd slowly. The dog does not bark and "charge" the herd. Why? Because this high level of control will increase defensiveness and the herd will scatter.

The same is true about initiating a confrontation. Start firmly enough to get the process started, but soft enough so as to not create too much defensiveness.

As the sheep start down the lane, they will test the fence. If they find it solid, they will resign themselves to moving toward the intended destination. If they find any other openings, they will take them. These shaky fence posts or openings are smoke screens that push your buttons and cause you to become defensive or to get off the issue.

People you are confronting will test you early in the process. If they find that you are solid, i.e., prepared to keep the interaction on one issue, calm, and respectful, they usually quit testing and move toward a clear "yes" or a clear "no" without conflict.

The strategies outlined in this chapter help you prepare the route and get your fence posts solid before you begin!

What Specifically Do You Want?

It is imperative that you determine your ultimate goal. I highly recommend that you *write* a Behavior Request Confrontation that is specific and have it critiqued by a peer or friend to ensure specificity. Use the worksheet in Figure 6-7, and refer to the steps for being specific listed in the Specific Desirable Behavior section of Chapter 6, The Progressive Confrontation Model.

It is my personal experience that if you are not absolutely specific, your confrontation has a low probability of being successful and a high probability of becoming a conflict.

Is the Return Worth the Investment?

Now that you have determined what you want in terms of behavior or behavior change, do a mental cost/benefit analysis.

What price are you going to pay?

- What is the risk to your relationship?
- Will there be some sort of retaliation?
- Will the person's behavior get worse, i.e., will he resist, perform less, withdraw, or get angrier?
- Do you want to take the time?

Really ask yourself, based on this objective, less emotional analysis, if this is really worth it. Often, we get caught up in the emotion or the "principle of the thing" and push ahead, when, in fact, it may be best to walk away, let it go, and accept it.

You might think of a modified version of the "Serenity Prayer": *"God, grant me the serenity to accept the things I cannot change **[or choose not to]**, the courage **[and skill]** to change the things I can, and the wisdom to know the difference."*

As I have prepared for a confrontation, I have found it helpful to ask myself, and even maybe others who know the person I'm planning to confront, *"Is there anything I can say or do that will get this person to change?"* If the answer is "no," I seriously consider letting it go. The only reason, at that point, for going ahead and confronting would be to prove to myself once and for all that I had tried and done everything I could do. Later, I would not wonder, *"What if I had tried?"*, and feel guilty for not having tried.

What Is the Worst Possible, Possible Scary Scenario?

Asking this question helps you get very clear about what you perceive to be the risk of making the confrontation. It requires courage and rigorous honesty on your part. It's like "taking the monster out of the closet," i.e., facing your worst fear.

If you make this confrontation, what are you afraid will happen? *"She will be hurt?" "He will not like you anymore?" "She will talk behind your back?" "He will go to your boss?" "She will retaliate?"*

Think out *"what am I afraid of?"* This fear is not right or wrong, good or bad, and it may or may not occur. But face it! This fear and the perceived risk is probably what has been keeping you from confronting this person.

Now, you should ask two other questions before you make any decision whether to confront:

1. Is this "worst possible scenario" real?

   What happens to any fear if we keep it inside? It gets bigger and bigger (the dinosaur gets bigger and more threatening).

   So, reality-check this fear. If necessary, reality-check it with someone in whom you can confide confidentially.

   If it isn't real, your fear and risk level goes down. If it is real, ask:

2. Can I live with this worst possible scenario?

   If you determine that the worst possible scenario is real and may happen, decide if you can live with this consequence. If you can, go ahead and prepare further. If you can't, stop here and start working on letting it go.

   It may take you some time and even a recurrence of the other person's undesirable behavior for you to make the decision.

   This worst possible scenario is a significant portion of the risk side of the cost/benefit analysis—*"Is it worth it?"*

What If You Get a "No?"

One of the risks of confrontation is that, by forcing the issue and, therefore, influencing more clear honesty and accountability by the other person, you may ultimately get a "no." It may take several tries on your part and/or the person may not give a clear verbal "no," but it will be clear that she is not going to do, at the moment, what you are requesting.

The ball is now back in your court. You now have to be willing to exercise another set of options:

- Are you going to walk away, and let it go and accept it?
- Are you going to try another personal power option (negotiate or confront) again?
- Are you going to describe the natural consequences?
- Are you going to use, or get access to, position power?

It is best if you have thought out what you may consider doing before you even begin the confrontation. Why?

1. The person may actually say during the confrontation, *"So, what are you going to do if I say 'no'?"* (kids are good at this one). It's a challenge to determine whether you are bluffing or are really prepared and maintain the integrity of your convictions. Is this confrontation of yours just an emotional response or is this issue really important to you?

2. Since the other person's "no" will force you to be more accountable, answering this question helps you determine what price you are willing to pay.

   Truly facing your potential accountability centers and grounds you, which results in your conveying more of a sense of calmness and focus.

   If you determine that you are not willing to tell the person the honest, natural consequences of his ultimate "no," or if you are unwilling or unable to use position power, this helps you understand that your confrontation will, at best, be an appeal and will remain at a low level of control. (For instance, you may start at the Discrepancy Confrontation or Behavior Request Confrontation level and not move to the Accountability Confrontation level.)

What Progressive Confrontation Level Should You Use to Start?

At what level of confrontation do you want to start the confrontation? Discrepancy Confrontation? Behavior Request Confrontation? Accountability Confrontation?

This depends on your relationship with the person, the level of risk you want to take, whether you have facts/data, how much choice you want to give her to dialogue, your past investment in trying to influence this person on this issue, your need to be in control of the process, or your urgency to address the issue.

There is no sure-fire guarantee. This is your best estimate of where to start based on your analysis and comfort level. If you err, it's probably best to err by starting at a softer, lower-risk level. You can always walk away and regroup or up the level.

Do You Have Specific Facts or Examples?

Since you have initiated the confrontation, most probably using a Behavior Request Confrontation, you have not yet told the person what he has done that is undesirable to you.

He may say . . .

> *"What did I do?"*
>
> *"What's the problem?"*
>
> *"I don't know what you are talking about."*
>
> *"That's not what happened."*
>
> *"I thought I was doing that!"*

Rarely in life do I ever say *never* or *always*, but this is one of those times. *Always* have two or three specific examples of the person's undesirable behavior so you are prepared if you encounter such a response.

Respond by saying: *"Let me give you an example."* Then describe an example of the undesirable behavior without using "blaming you" or judgmentalness.

For instance, using the example from above, if the person responded:
> *"I don't know what you're talking about."*

You would say:
> *"Let me give you an example. Yesterday, when you finished your work and went home, there was no offer to help me."*

It is my experience that without two or three specific examples of what the other person has said or done (or not said or done), you will encounter problems and, in fact, will fail. If you don't have these examples, I would recommend not confronting except at a Discrepancy Confrontation level.

Imagine this dialogue:

You: *"I need you to be on time every day."*

Her: *"I have been."*

You have a *tie* regarding your perceptions. She perceives there is no problem, you perceive that there is. There is only one option that may settle a difference of perceptions. *Data and facts! Without them, you are lost!*

What "No" Behavior Do You Expect?

You know this person, so you may very well know how he might react. Angry? Intimidating? Surprised? Confused? Hurt? Defensive? Resistant? Denying? Changing the subject? Silence? Ask yourself, *"What three adjectives would describe how I think he might react if I confront?"*

To the degree you can get ready for any of these possible reactions, you can unhook your dinosaur brain and rewire your buttons so they don't get pushed. Remember, if his reaction is not a "yes," it has some "no" in it. Your task is to not let the verbal/emotional component of the "no" get you off the issue.

How Will You Respond?

For the less difficult "nos," you have already learned your options:

- dialogue
- negotiate
- up the level of control
- describe the natural consequences
- walk away and accept it

For the more difficult "nos," those that you have determined may push your buttons and get you to react and be a dinosaur, more specific options are covered in Chapter 8, Dealing With Difficult Emotional Reactions. Specific strategies are offered for dealing with anger, intimidation, crying, silence, and the person physically walking away.

How Much Time Will You Spend With the "No?"

To prevent the possibility of going on and on with the confrontation and interaction, try to decide how much time you will spend if you get a "no" before exercising your next option. During this time you will stay silent and, thus, not react to the verbal/emotional response. Two rules of thumb might help:

1. The more risk and vulnerability you feel, the less time you will spend. The risk here means that you are vulnerable to getting your buttons pushed. The less risk and vulnerability you feel, the more time you might spend.

2. The less important the relationship to you, the less time you will spend. The more important the relationship, the more time you may be willing to spend.

In either case, pick an amount of time. It's like setting a mental time clock (15 seconds? 30 seconds? 5 minutes? a week?). It's up to you! Typically, if there is perceived risk, you might consider 15 to 30 seconds. This 15- to 30-second time frame is not sacred. The amount of time you wait needs to be enough to allow the other person to react, vent, and be emotional and hopefully then calm down, as long as you can give this time without reacting yourself (see Chapter 8 for more details).

What Will Your Next Strategy Be?

Again, be prepared. You have initiated your confrontation at one of the three levels of the Progressive Confrontation Model. You have gotten "no" behavior; you have waited your predetermined time so your buttons have not been pushed. Now, what's next?

The possibilities are:
- Use a negotiation question.
- Use another confrontation level.
- Describe the natural consequences.
- Walk away and accept it.
- Give brief, honest, respectful responses

I suggest you have another option ready before you begin your confrontation. Hopefully, you won't need a next option, but if you do, you will be ready.

Reminder: You may not remember, but one of the reasons given for always writing out a Behavior Request Confrontation, no matter what level of progressive confrontation you use, is that you may get "lost" during the confrontation . . . sort of like stage fright! With all your preparation, you may still go blank or get discombobulated. If that happens—and it has to me—you can always "be a broken record" and repeat your Behavior Request Confrontation; it's your life raft or safety net if all else fails.

Would It Help to Put Your Confrontation in Context?

Frequently it works best if you get right to the issue and deliver your confrontation—no small talk, no lengthy lead-in, no telling why you are confronting (leads to discussion of undesirable behavior). Just:

"I need you to _____ *."*

or

"I have a problem and I need your help; I would like you to
_____ *."*

Small talk only heightens the tension. The other person senses something important is about to happen, so go for it! Proceed immediately with the confrontation.

Yet there are a number of times when you could preface your confrontation with a brief contextual statement that might improve the chance that the person will hear you and not react defensively (**D↗T↘**). Often I have found that sharing my feelings about the importance of the relationship has been a good way to start a confrontation. For instance, if the person you are about to confront feels inadequate and often overreacts and overblows the issue, you might say,

> *"I have an issue I need to discuss. Before I do, I want you to know I value you and the relationship and don't want to harm the relationship. I need you to listen and help me resolve this issue. I need you to*
> _____.*"*

Are You Confronting the Right Person First?

Is the person you are confronting going to, as a result of your confronting her, run to another person in your life who might become her ally, perhaps not support you, and cause you problems? Will she involve another person who will take her side and who has the position power and/or influence with you to get you to fold your tent?

Often, this other person is someone who has position power over you, such as a boss. Another example is a child running to your spouse.

If there may be such a third party out there and if the person you are confronting may likely go to her as a way of not complying with your request, I seriously suggest that you go to this third party first, as a prevention, to request that she act in a way that enables you to deal with the person and issue without complication. Make a direct Behavior Request Confrontation to this person regarding the behavior you would like her to agree to if the confronted person comes to her.

For example:

> *"I would like you to, if (name) comes to you, to stay out of it, not discuss it, and send her back to me."*
>
> or
>
> *"I need you, if (name) comes to you regarding my confrontation, to only discuss it with her if I am present."*
>
> or
>
> *"I need to know if you are willing to make a commitment to me to support me in my request of (name), 'yes' or 'no'?"*

Notice that you can make this kind of request without betraying the details of any sensitive, private, and/or confidential issue.

If the person you need support from is your boss, it is often helpful to describe the details so she has some feel for the situation and, thus, will not be surprised later.

If this third party will not agree to stay out of the issue, I would strongly suggest you reconsider your confrontation until she does. This third party constitutes an escape for the person you are confronting. Sometimes there are several people that you need to "align" before you can hope to be successful with your confrontation.

Now, using the real confrontation you wrote in all three confrontation formats in Chapter 6, complete the Confrontation Strategy Worksheet (Figure 7-1).

Writing your confrontation specifically and in the appropriate confrontation format was the first step in getting ready to confront. The second step in your preparation involved thinking through your strategy.

Your next step, if you have decided that you might get an intense reaction from the other person, is to have the skills to deal with various difficult emotional reactions.

Confrontation Strategy Worksheet

1. What Do I Want? *(Write your request in a Behavior Request Confrontation format)*:

    I _____

    (degree of control/choice word or phrase)

    you to _____

    (desired behavior with specificity)

    _____

    _____

    _____

    _____

    and, as a result _____

    _____

    (consequence/result)

2. Is It Worth Doing? ❑ Yes ❑ No

3. What's the WPPSS/Risk? _____

    _____

    (a) Is the WPPSS Real? ❑ Yes ❑ No   (b) Can I Live With This Risk? ❑ Yes ❑ No

4. What Am I Going to Do If I Get a "No?" _____

    _____

5. At What Confrontation Level Am I Going to Begin?

    ❑ Discrepancy ❑ Behavior Request ❑ Accountability

6. Do I Have Specific Facts or Examples of the Undesirable Behavior If Needed?

    1. _____

    2. _____

7. What "No" Behavior Do I Expect?

    ❑ Anger ❑ Blaming ❑ Confusion ❑ Hurt ❑ Silence ❑ Others _____

8. How Will I Respond to This Expected "No" Behavior? _____

9. How Much Time Will I Spend With This "No" Behavior? _____

10. What Confrontation or "No" Strategy Will I Move to If I Get a "No" to My Initial

    Confrontation? _____

11. Will Putting My Confrontation into Context Help?

    ❑ Yes ❑ No

12. Am I Confronting the Right Person First?

    ❑ Yes ❑ No

    If Not, Who or Which People Do I Need to Confront First? _____

Figure 7-1

CHAPTER 8

Dealing With Difficult Emotional Reactions

Imagine a person in your life with whom you currently have, or have had, a lot of difficulty dealing. Whatever he did, you felt reactive, emotional, or irrational.

As you think of such a person, you have probably asked yourself (and probably lost sleep over), *"Why do I get so out-of-sorts?"* Most of us, at least initially, when someone's behavior bothers us, try to identify some part of the other person's behavior that is the problem and place the blame on him:

- He is too opinionated.

- He is a whiner.

- He is just an angry person.

- He will not listen.

Guess what? The other person's reactive behavior may be the catalyst, but somehow his behavior pushes our buttons in such a way that we begin to react in some ineffective manner. The problem is not the other person, he is not the issue, it is us . . . our reaction.

"I have met the enemy and he is us."

—Walt Kelley
Pogo, 1970

There are some "no" behaviors that each of us, based on our unique experience and makeup, have special difficulty handling. A behavior that pushes your buttons may not be the same behavior that another person finds difficult.

Lots of people have difficulty with an angry reaction. Others have difficulty with crying and pained behavior. My personal nemesis is a silent, withdrawn, pouting reaction.

Frequently it is the people closest to us who unintentionally say and do things that push our buttons. Consequently, we often react more to those we love than to strangers. It is maddening to feel this emotional loss of control with our loved ones.

I love my two children and the feeling is mutual. We are all good, caring people. Yet, even though they are grown and married and have their own lives, certain of their behaviors "hook" me. As I have examined these behaviors, I am very aware now that it is a certain, specific behavior, rather than a person, that elicits my reaction, because I find myself reacting, although not as intensely, to anyone who behaves in this manner. The problem is me, my reaction to a behavior, not the other person. I need to rewire these buttons.

One of the behaviors that I react to is withdrawn silence. I make a request or ask a question and the other person doesn't verbally respond. I have become aware that my immediate reaction is to feel unworthy and not liked. This is probably not the intent of the behavior, but it is my automatic reaction. I then either get intense, pushy, annoyed, or withdrawn. None of these reactions lead to effective communication and relating at that moment.

I have had to learn to suspend this immediate frame-of-reference reaction and to substitute some new thoughts and behaviors, such as not taking it personally. I am not as effective reacting this new way as I would like to be, but I am better than I used to be. I have to be satisfied with, and focus on, progress.

I have also become aware that I probably developed this reaction (becoming annoyed or withdrawing) to this particular behavior (silence) when I was a young child and that it became a habit. It probably helped me cope with the behavior of certain adults when I was young, but is not effective now that I am an adult who has more effective options.

Based on my experience, and the experience of the people I have worked with who have learned to deal effectively with tense emotional reactions, it seems that the other person's emotional behavior hooks some unhealthy part of us, perhaps our inadequacy, powerlessness, fear, shame, or hurt.

People often report that the emotional reaction that triggers them is one that their parents, siblings, or people who were significant in their upbringing used to influence them and may still use. It is important to stay out of the judgment business at this point. People's behavior is not right or wrong.

Recent advances in the studies of "co-dependency" and family systems seem to indicate that children learn certain coping mechanisms to deal with and survive dysfunction in their family of origin. These behaviors, such as anger, shame, or withdrawing, enabled the child to react and survive, but become habits. Now, as an adult, the same reaction occurs when encountering a stressful, button-pushing experience. Yet this old, once-useful behavior is not very effective and healthy today. So the old reaction needs to be unwired and a new, more effective option substituted. There are many books, resources, and counseling services available on this subject if further information is desired. One such book is *Healing the Shame That Binds You* by John Bradshaw.

The only issue here is to learn new options to be able to respond to these behaviors in a healthier way. Remember, the irrational response would be to continue to *react* the same old way. This too is an option, although it is assumed, since you are reading this book, that you want to learn new options.

Being effective at dealing with these especially difficult emotional behaviors requires that you:

1. Be rigorously honest with yourself.
2. Stop blaming the other person.
3. Identify what part of you is tweaked (even if you can't figure this out yet, you can learn).
4. Learn a new verbal response.

So, in essence, you rewire the button so your old reaction does not automatically occur. You circumvent your dinosaur-brain reaction by creating a new verbal/emotional response that is programmed into and uses your cortex.

In the beginning, people literally have to practice, rehearse, and almost mechanically use the new response. It seems to take this kind of fortitude, commitment, and practice to override the old long-standing, automatic, emotional reaction.

Be patient with yourself! You have had years of practice the old way. Your old button will get pushed from time to time, especially by those closest to you, such as your children. I'm sure you have heard the expression, "His daughter has him wrapped around her little finger." His daughter exhibits behavior that pushes his buttons!

Not immediately reacting sends a very clear message that you are in control of the process and that emotional, reactive behavior will not work!

The key is to not let the other person's behavior work—that is, to get you to react. With most emotional reactions, if you can avoid being reactive, getting your buttons pushed, or getting off the issue for approximately 30 seconds, the other person calms down.

Now, you probably have an idea about which emotional reactions cause you problems. Let's examine a few and some options for how to respond to each. There seem to be two steps people use to rewire their responses:

1. Don't respond immediately at all. Silence is marvelous. Program yourself to not respond at all for 5 to 10 seconds or, in the face of intense anger (see the next section), 15 to 30 seconds.

2. Respond with a brief, honest, respectful response (introduced in Chapter 5): *"That's not the issue." "Yes, that's true." "No, that's not true." "We will deal with that later."*

These responses should be given calmly, almost matter-of-factly. Don't go on and on or get drawn into a dialogue.

Brief, Honest, Respectful Responses to Emotional Reactions

You have delivered your initial confrontation and the person's reaction is:

(Indignant):
"Well, you do the same thing!"

Your Response:
"That's not the issue."

(Hurt):
"You just don't like me."

Your Response:
"That's not true."

(Defensive):
"You're not so perfect yourself. I have something I'm not so happy with you about."

Your Response:
"We will deal with that later. That's not the issue now."

Figure 8-1

These brief, honest, respectful responses may be used with, and are usually effective with, any emotional reaction. In fact, once you become accustomed to using them, you will find that they become automatic and will frequently begin to slip into other day-to-day interactions.

Gore-Tex® Analogy

Gore-Tex is a clothing material that keeps the rain and wind out, but breathes, so air gets in and body moisture gets out.

It is important that you let your request out (breathe), but do not let the "wind and rain" (the other person's potentially emotional, hurtful response) in.

If, during the confrontation, the other person does not express excess emotion, it's like a nice day and you don't need Gore-Tex. At that point, the two of you can dialogue and negotiate without any special protection.

If there is bad weather (the other person's excess emotional response), you need protection. Brief silence and the brief, honest, respectful responses can be your Gore-Tex—your protection—until the person calms down.

There are some emotional reactions that can be even more effectively dealt with using more tailored strategies. These emotional reactions include anger, silence, crying, physically walking away, and/or threat of physical harm.

Anger

You confront and the other person reacts angrily. His anger works and you are not effective at being in control of the process if you 1) react by getting defensive, angry, or off the issue, or 2) get intimidated or "fold your tent" and back off. If you do either, you don't deal with the issue, and his anger, in essence, worked; it prevented him from having to deal effectively and you either went away or became a hurtful dinosaur. He can then be angry at you and justify not being rational and open to being influenced.

Angry people will react angrily. It's their habit or mode of operation. Once you confront, they don't call a time-out and use their cortex. They don't decide which way they want to react—hurt or angry or whiny or rational. They just react from their dinosaur brain. The angry person usually reacts angrily, the whiny person whines, et cetera.

The other person's reaction is not right or wrong, it just is! Don't try to diagnose it or figure out why. *Just don't let the emotional reaction push your buttons and get YOUR dinosaur brain reacting!*

People behave the way they do because it works!

There are many options to use with anger, but I have found the following to be especially effective:

- Don't respond verbally. Stay silent for 15 to 30 seconds or until the anger begins to subside.
- If the anger decreases, repeat your original request.
- If the anger continues longer than 30 seconds, you have a choice: either reschedule or allow more time.
- If you reschedule, do so in a respectful manner that describes a time that you will meet (confront) again and does not accuse, judge, or blame.

One way to understand an angry reaction is to imagine that the person has a fuel tank inside and that the anger being expressed is like a raging fire. Like many types of fires, anger needs oxygen to keep it going. There are only two sources of oxygen in this interaction: what comes out of the other person's mouth and what comes out of yours. Imagine that when you say anything, you are a "bellows" stoking the fire. Almost anything you say—whether it is compassionate, empathic, or a question—has a high probability of causing the fire to flare! So, this strategy is intended to starve the fire. When the fuel tank runs down, the anger should subside.

Let's assume you have just made a Behavior Request Confrontation and that the other person reacted angrily. You have remained silent for 30 seconds while the venting continued and you sense that it is best to reschedule. An effective response might be:

> *"Apparently this is a very emotional issue, so I will restate my request tomorrow morning right before work."*

You have not blamed and there is a specific time. The person hopefully realizes that he did not avoid dealing with the issue, that it is not going away, and his anger did not work.

When you reschedule, be careful that you are not running from the issue and have not implied blame. What two things are wrong with the following response?

> *"Obviously you are real emotional about this issue, so we will deal with it later when you have had a chance to calm down."*

First, it is "blaming you," and second, it is open-ended and not rescheduled.

Often, when you leave an issue open-ended, the other person walks away perceiving that it is over, that, in essence, the issue has gone away. His behavior worked! Guess what? His behavior is still a problem, he will be better at anger the next time, and you are more resentful and so will be less apt to confront or to do so effectively next time.

If there is a threat, or you suspect the possibility of physical harm, please see the section on Threat of Physical Harm later in this chapter.

Silence

You have confronted and the other person is silent. Her silence works if you start talking. Remember, she is comfortable with silence, it is her normal reaction. Since you are not as comfortable with silence, especially during this risky, emotional time, you may automatically start talking. Guess what? Her silence pushed your buttons and you have started to react verbally. When you begin to fill this tense silence, two problems occur: She is not *having* to respond to your request, and what you say is not thought out and will probably contain "blaming you," accusations of "wrong" behavior, and other irrelevant issues.

So, how do you best handle a silent reaction? I suggest the following:

- Stay silent for 15 to 30 seconds. Let the tension build. If, after 30 seconds, you have still not gotten a response, say, *"I assume your silence, at the moment, is a 'no'."*

My experience has been that you will now get a response; now you are on your verbal way.

Crying, Pain, Whining, Fragility

When you confront a person and she cries and is in pain, what is your typical reaction? If you are not careful, you will react by immediately reaching out physically or verbally to soothe or decrease her pain by softening your request. At that moment, the crying has worked: You have begun to fold. Why this reaction? Probably because you felt responsible for the other person's pain, that you caused it! If you used these confrontation skills, you have not caused the pain. There is a difference between you causing the pain and the other person feeling pained. If your confrontation involved "blaming you," judgment, describing the wrong behavior, or excess emotion, you may have partly caused the pain. But if you made a Behavior Request Confrontation, as outlined in this book, you did not cause the pain. The pain is the other person's immediate, and usually normal, reaction. She has a right to the reaction, but it should not keep you from sticking, respectfully, with the original issue or request.

In many ways, dealing effectively with pain and crying is similar to dealing with anger. Don't let either emotion push your buttons. In fact, I suggest you deal with crying almost exactly the way I recommend dealing with anger:

- Don't respond verbally. Stay silent for 15 to 30 seconds or until her crying begins to subside.
- If the pain or crying decreases, repeat your original request.
- If the crying continues longer than 30 seconds, you have a choice: either reschedule or give her more time.
- If you reschedule, do so in a respectful manner that describes a time that you will meet (confront) again and does not accuse, judge, or blame.

There is one additional option in dealing with crying. Whereas I recommended not responding with empathy to anger, responding with empathy to pain may show the compassion you want to express. Be aware, though, that when you deliver empathy, the crying may intensify or take longer.

Physically Walking Away

Occasionally when you confront someone, the person will walk away before you have achieved resolution. Walking away is a pretty clear "no" at the moment. Your task, as in dealing with all "no" behavior, is to not let this behavior work.

So, what do you do? I suggest, in almost all cases, that you plan to follow up with a repeat confrontation in the near future—an hour or more later in the day, or the next day. This persistence delivers a clear message that the behavior did not work and that you are committed.

Another option when you are actually experiencing this walking-away behavior is to say something at that moment. Some verbal responses that you might consider are:

> *"I'll take this as a 'no'."*

> *"I'll repeat my request again later today."*

> *"This is not finished. I will make this request (specify when)."*

Making this type of response lets the person know that the behavior did not work. Often he will reconsider and deal with the issue.

Another option is, before making your confrontation, to make a brief contextual statement that would ask him to not walk away. For instance:

> *"This is a very important issue to me, so I would like you to stay and help me resolve it and not walk away. I would like you to (your request)."*

Although you may be tempted, especially with children, to physically restrain the person, I would not recommend doing so.

If you do have position power, you might want to state, contextually, that walking away will be considered an act of insubordination.

Threat of Physical Harm

If, when preparing for a confrontation, you sense or intuit (have a feeling) there may be potential physical harm, *do not do it* using these guidelines.

If during a confrontation there is a real or perceived threat of physical harm, *remove yourself* immediately.

In either case, special skills and strategies are required to approach such a person. Please consult with a professional for help. In your personal life, this may be a counselor. In the work setting, it may be your supervisor, the employee assistance program, or the personnel department, depending on the situation.

Now you have all the conceptual understanding necessary to be able to conduct a real and effective confrontation using this new approach. Yet, as with any skill, translating this understanding into a more natural, automatic set of behaviors requires practice. Chapter 9 provides a guide to practicing the real confrontation to readiness.

CHAPTER 9

Practicing Your Confrontation

Now that you have written your confrontation and developed a strategy, it is time to practice.

Up to this point in your learning process, this confrontation skill is still intellectual or theoretical. You probably believe, or hope, based on what you have learned, that you will be able to remain calm and rational and to keep the issue on *one* issue, *your* issue, and move toward a "yes." But how can you gain more confidence?

The Practice Process

Over the years of trying to help people learn this confrontation skill, the most difficult aspect has been learning to unhook the emotional buttons involved in the issue or situation. This practice process has evolved as an effective way to face the potential emotional risk involved in the situation you are to confront. It is very simple, but not easy!

Schedule a Practice Situation

Choose a person in your life who you trust, is willing to help, and will honor your confidentiality (a friend, peer, spouse, even an older child). Share three adjectives that describe how you think the person you are planning to confront might react—angry, annoyed, confused, hurt, defensive, silent, agreeable, et cetera. Ask them to role-play this emotional response to the best of their ability. They do not have to be a professional actor. Their task is to try to push your buttons using the emotional responses you describe. It may help them if you briefly describe the situation, but this is not mandatory. Choose a location that ensures privacy.

Memorize Your Initial Confrontation

From your Confrontation Worksheet (see Figures 6-7, 6-9, and 6-11), memorize your initial confrontation. You are ready when you can deliver this confrontation while maintaining steady eye contact with your practice partner.

A "trick" that sometimes helps is to write down your confrontation on a small card or piece of paper and put it in your pocket, day-minder, or purse. Do not take it out, but visualize the words if you forget.

Set a Positive Tone Non-Verbally

Ask yourself what message you want your non-verbal behavior to deliver before you even open your mouth to articulate your request. Preferably you want your body language and facial expression to send the same message as the words you have prepared (confident, prepared, urgent, focused, sincere, and caring).

There is a non-verbal posture called **attending behavior** that can help you deliver this non-verbal message. Effective attending behavior includes having an *open face*, having a *squared shoulder plane* with the other person, having an *appropriate distance* from the other person, and *leaning forward (inclined posture)*.

Open Face
You should have a facial expression that communicates the lights are on and there *is* someone who is home, open, focused, confident, while relaxed, caring, and not frowning.

Squared Shoulder Plane
You should face the person squarely, your shoulder plane parallel to his.

Appropriate Distance
The distance between your head and the other person's should be approximately 2 to 3 feet. To get a feel for this distance, be aware of the distance between you and another person when you are standing talking to her. This is also the appropriate space when exhibiting good attending behavior while you are sitting. It may feel too close at first, but remember the message you are trying to convey, the importance of the issue, and your confidence!

Leaning Forward (Inclined Posture)

It is very important that you lean forward throughout your confrontation. This delivers a message of caring, urgency, and confidence. You might try leaning forward so that your arms are on your thighs or the arms of a chair or a table. Thus, your weight will be off your back. This attending posture should be relaxed, not rigid and tense, but solid. You should begin the confrontation with good attending behavior and remain in this posture throughout. If you begin to lean back, it will be a signal to yourself that you are becoming defensive, reactive, and unsure. Believe me, the other person will also notice.

Deliver Your Confrontation and Practice Your Responses

Now you are ready to begin your practice. Deliver your confrontation to your practice partner. When he responds, role-playing his emotional response, don't react. Use brief silence and brief, honest, respectful responses to keep control of the process. If you become shaky, lost, or emotional, stop and discuss what response you could have used to keep control of the process. Keep practicing, over and over again, until you feel ready. Then go initiate the real confrontation.

There is no standard amount of practice. Each person differs depending on the risk, issue, person, and situation. I have had people who needed to practice dozens of times over months to be ready. Others need one or two practices over 20 minutes. The key is to practice until you feel ready.

Now, you are nearly ready to use your new confrontation skills. You have prepared and practiced and have considered all the negative things that may go wrong and cause you to potentially lose control of the influencing process.

Are you ready to deal with success? Your goal *is* to get a "yes" or a clear "no" to your request. When you get a "yes," remember that this is a verbal "yes." You may need to assist the other person to change to the requested behavior. Chapter 10 discusses Changing Behavior.

CHAPTER 10

Changing Behavior

Confrontation is hopefully the start of a change process. You have requested a change and the other person may or may not agree. If she gives you a "yes" and agrees, please understand that the change process has just begun. The confrontation is necessary, but by itself is usually not enough to result in long-term behavior change. You may need to follow up her "yes" with a W^4 (who, what, where, when, and how).

Often, because the confrontation is risky and emotional, when we get a verbal "yes," we experience such relief that we don't push ahead to ensure the verbal "yes" will be followed by a behavioral change.

People don't just change behavior because they agree to. Change takes hard work, discipline, and always some personalized feeling of accountability.

Given that you are satisfied with the extent (percentage) of "yes" in the response, I suggest you thank the person for her help and then specifically reiterate what is to follow. For example, assuming you finally got a "yes" from the confrontation, you might say:

> *"Thanks. To reiterate, you have agreed, starting today, to _____. I really appreciate your understanding and will-ingness to help me. I know this is not easy for either of us. If this doesn't happen, I will respectfully remind you of your agreement."*

Often, the behavior that you are requesting will require the other person to change an old, long-standing habit. For many of us, changing an old habit is difficult because the old habit is something we say or do without conscious awareness of doing it. How is another person going to change a behavior if she is not aware of when she does it? Perhaps it's a word, or voice tone, or a raise of the eyebrow, or a whiny voice. She is not even aware of doing it! In these cases, you might try one of the strategies outlined below. They are based on the fact that people who are attempting to change an old habit or behavior are usually not immediately aware when this old, automatic behavior occurs and, thus, need an aid to increasing their awareness at that moment. Once they begin to be aware of the old behavior as it occurs, they begin to substitute the new behavior.

Behavior Contract

This is a strategy that the two of you agree to try. The other person is open to your help and you are willing to help.

The agreement involves your giving a discreet signal when the other person exhibits the old habit or behavior. The signal could be anything, for instance, a tap of the wrist, touching your ear lobe, a wink, a time-out sign. This signal helps the person gain an awareness when the old habit occurs. Over time, he begins to gain self-awareness and to substitute the new behavior for the old.

Frequent Feedback

You might agree to give feedback frequently, for instance daily, to discuss progress. This discussion should be brief and requires that you give specific examples describing when the person exhibited or did not exhibit the new agreed-upon behavior. Be sure to reinforce or give positive feedback for incidence of the desired behavior and for trying to change.

Observe the Undesirable and/or Desirable Behavior

Instead of you helping the person gain the awareness of her behavior, this option places the accountability on her. She agrees to tabulate or keep score of her behavior. A version of this strategy is used in almost all weight-control programs. People count calories or weigh food or list what they have eaten. The idea is to ensure that the person has frequent awareness of the old habit.

An interesting thing happens when we keep score (stay aware) of the old behavior—it has a tendency to decrease! Have the person agree to keep her own score. Some examples are keeping a tally on a sheet on the refrigerator or keeping a notepad tally on her desk or calendar.

Whatever method you adopt, frequently discuss and reinforce progress.

You now have all the skills needed to confront effectively. You can *write and articulate* your Confrontation Request with specificity, you can *develop a strategy* to lessen conflict and keep control of the process, and you can *practice your confrontation* to increase your skill.

Now, you have to decide whether the specific confrontation is worth it. If it is, proceed. If not, begin the process of letting it go!

The next chapter contains two sample confrontations for your review. They may help you bring together the entire process.

CHAPTER 11

Bringing It All Together

The following confrontation examples are offered to summarize the entire process. They were real situations.

Remember that the people actually confronting did so from their frame of reference, not yours. Based on their individual values, urgency, willingness to invest, risk level, and caring, they confronted as described. Don't judge their process. You may, in a similar situation, choose to start at a different level of confrontation or to influence with a different level of control.

Yet, please note that they both maintained the integrity of the confrontation process as described. They were not hurtful and they kept control of the process by keeping the conversation on one issue—theirs—and moving toward a "yes"!

Example 1

A 31-year-old woman, married for a number of years, with two school-age children, lives in the Northwest, but was born and raised in the Midwest where her mother continues to reside. This woman had gone to college, raised a family, worked in a professional capacity, and, in her own mind and in others', has done well.

Her concern focused on her mother not being positive or supportive, and in not showing interest in her feelings, aspirations, and accomplishments. During telephone conversations and occasional visits, she reported that her mother never said anything positive and frequently was critical of her parenting, marriage, and house decorating.

She had been festering for a number of years, had occasionally blown up at her mother, and now felt angry and powerless about doing anything that might influence a change in her mother.

Using the Confrontation Strategy Worksheet described in Chapter 7, she prepared for a possible confrontation.

The undesirable behavior was her mother being critical and judgmental of her lifestyle and her mother's lack of positive support. She explored several influencing options, including all three confrontation formats. She also agonized over the potential negative consequences to her relationship with her mother.

Please note the number of options used as the interaction proceeds, including putting the confrontation in context, two levels of confrontation (Discrepancy and Behavior Request), delivering high levels of the Core Dimensions (empathy), brief, honest, respectful responses, and getting a commitment (W^4) to the "yes."

Confrontation Strategy Worksheet

1. What Do I Want? (Write your request in a Behavior Request Confrontation format):

   I _____ *would like* _____
   ### (degree of control/choice word or phrase)

   you to, *when we talk, to say positive things about me, my family, and our lifestyle instead of being critical. For example, to say things like, "You do a good job parenting the children," "How's your job going?", and "I appreciate the time you have taken off to be with me." If you have something critical to say, please do so when we are in private and after you have thought it out.*
   ### (desired behavior with specificity)

   If you will honor this request, *I will feel that you care and I will want to spend more time with you."*
   ### (consequence/result)

2. Is It Worth Doing? ☑ Yes   ☐ No

3. What's the WPPSS/Risk? <u>That mother will be hurt and withdrawn, and will disconnect from us (choose to spend less time with us).</u>

   (a) Is the WPPSS Real? ☑ Yes   ☐ No

   (b) Can I Live With This Risk? ☑ Yes   ☐ No

4. What Am I Going to Do If I Get a "No?" <u>Tell her the consequences of her behavior (that I will spend less time with her).</u>

5. At What Confrontation Level Am I Going to Begin?

   ☑ Discrepancy ☐ Behavior Request ☐ Accountability

6. Do I Have Specific Facts or Examples of the Undesirable Behavior If Needed?

   1. *Two weeks ago during a telephone conversation she said, "You don't spend enough time with the children."*

   2. *During her recent visit, she made derogatory comments about me and my husband two times.*

7. What "No" Behavior Do I Expect?

   ☐ Anger ☐ Blaming ☐ Confusion ☑ Hurt ☐ Silence ☑ Others *Defensive*

8. How Will I Respond to This Expected "No" Behavior? *Stay silent; show empathy.*

9. How Much Time Will I Spend With This "No" Behavior? *Several minutes if she cries.*

10. What Confrontation or "No" Strategy Will I Move to If I Get a "No" to My Initial Confrontation?

    State that her response is a "no" and tell her the natural consequences.

11. Will Putting My Confrontation into Context Help? *Yes, I will start by telling her I value the relationship and want a good relationship.*

12. Am I Confronting the Right Person First? ☑ Yes   ☐ No

    If Not, Who or Which People Do I Need to Confront First? _____

Figure 11-1

This is the report on how the confrontation went:

Daughter (nervous, but calm and serious with good attending behavior): *"Mom, I love you and want to have a good relationship with you and I want you to spend time with me and my family. There is one issue that I need help with. I would like you to listen and try to understand.*

I'm confused because on the one hand you love me and I know that, while on the other hand I'm frequently criticized for how I conduct my life and rarely receive positive support."

Mother (silence, non-verbally exhibiting some surprised embarrassment): *"Yes, I do love you, but I'm not critical. I just want the best for you."*

Daughter (after 3 to 5 seconds of silence): *"I appreciate that, but that's not the issue."*

Mother (with a hint of defensive anger): *"You never would do what I wanted—only listened to your father. I tried to teach you how to cook and raise a family, but you always had to resist. You were never interested in what I felt was important!"*

Daughter (calmly): *"That's not true."*

Mother (with tears): *"You don't want me around. You just put up with me."*

Daughter: *"So, you're hurt because you think we don't care about you."*

Mother (more tears, but calmer): *"I get so angry at myself because I'm so critical. I'm doing the same things with your sister. I care, but I don't know how to show it."*

Daughter: *"What would help me and what I would like you to do when we talk, is to say positive things about me, my family, and our lifestyle instead of being critical. For example, to say things like, "You do a good job parenting the children," "How's your job going?", and "I appreciate the time you have taken off to be with me." If you have something critical to say, please do so when we are in private and after you have thought it out."*

Mother (softly): *"I'll try."*

Daughter (softly and taking mother's hands): *"Mom, I appreciate your willingness to try. I know this is not easy, but I need us both to try to demonstrate more caring and your agreeing to do this will really help. From now on, you've agreed to say positive things and, if you have a problem with me or my life, will either not say anything or come to me in private to discuss it with concern and without judgment. If you make a critical remark in the future, I will take you aside and remind you of your agreement."*

They hug.

Example 2

Glen, having become part of his current work team about six months ago, was quite frustrated and discouraged by the negative attitude of some of his co-workers. One in particular seemed to be the catalyst for much gossip, rumor spreading, and being critical of the organization, bosses, and other staff in general. Although Glen was a peer with the same job classification as Bob, this informal leader, he had not been in the organization nearly as long.

Although other staff usually went along with, and participated in, the gossip and stories, Glen sensed that they too were quite uncomfortable with the inappropriateness of the behavior and were, in fact, a little intimidated by Bob. Glen's boss was not perceived as a strong supervisor and was also perceived as being hesitant to confront Bob.

Glen attempted to tolerate the atmosphere, but was becoming increasingly discouraged, to the point of considering quitting.

Glen decided to confront Bob, knowing that he had questionable support from above, but that he might receive support from other team members. Glen's daily quality of life was obviously very important to him. He was also quite skilled and could easily obtain a similar job elsewhere. Thus, quitting was not as risky to him as it may be for many of us.

Confrontation Strategy Worksheet

1. What Do I Want? (Write your request in a Behavior Request Confrontation format):

    I _____ *need* _____
    (degree of control/choice word or phrase)

    you to *exhibit a more positive attitude during work hours; by that I mean, if you have a problem with another person or group, going to that person or group to address the issue instead of talking negatively about them in public or behind their back to other staff.*
    (desired behavior with specificity)

    Also, if you do, *I will have more respect for you and there will be a more positive team atmosphere.*
    (consequence/result)

2. Is It Worth Doing? ☑ Yes   ☐ No

3. What's the WPPSS/Risk? *He will laugh at me and I will become the focus of his jokes and judgments. It will get worse and I may have to quit.*

    (a) Is the WPPSS Real? ☑ Yes   ☐ No

    (b) Can I Live With This Risk? ☑ Yes   ☐ No

4. What Am I Going to Do If I Get a "No"? *Tell him that I am going to resign and that if and when I do, I will first go to upper management to tell them the reason.*

5. At What Confrontation Level Am I Going to Begin?
    ☐ Discrepancy ☑ Behavior Request ☐ Accountability

6. Do I Have Specific Facts or Examples of the Undesirable Behavior If Needed?
    1. *Friday, at the lunch table in front of the team, he called our supervisor gutless and the*
        organization manipulative.

    2. *Thursday he made two racial remarks about an employee from another team.*

7. What "No" Behavior Do I Expect?
    ☑ Anger   ☑ Blaming ☐ Confusion ☐ Hurt ☐ Silence ☑ Others *Verbal Retaliation*

8. How Will I Respond to This Expected "No" Behavior? *Silence, then reschedule if it continues.*

9. How Much Time Will I Spend With This "No" Behavior? *Up to 5 minutes.*

10. What Confrontation or "No" Strategy Will I Move to If I Get a "No" to My Initial Confrontation?
    Tell him the natural consequences.

11. Will Putting My Confrontation into Context Help?
    Yes, I will indicate that I want a good relationship with him and that he is a good worker. I value being part of a cooperative team and organization.

12. Am I Confronting the Right Person First? ☐ Yes   ☑ No
    If Not, Who or Which People Do I Need to Confront First?
    I will tell our supervisor that I am going to confront and that if it does not work I would like him to confront Bob next.

Figure 11-2

This is the report on how the confrontation went:

Glen (calmly): *"I value you as a worker and your expertise in this business. I would like to be able to work with you and have a good, supportive working relationship. I have a problem that I need help with.*

I need you to exhibit a more positive attitude during work hours; by that I mean, if you have a problem with another person or group, going to that person or group to address the issue instead of talking negatively about them in public or behind their back to other staff. Also, if you do, I will have more respect for you and there will be a more positive team atmosphere."

Bob (angry and defensive): *"Who do you think you are? You don't know how bad it really is and how incompetent management is around here! You come waltzing in with your harebrained ideas about teamwork without knowing that we have tried and management just does their thing! Did you know that right before you came two people were fired for no reason whatsoever? You know why? So the organization could meet their cultural diversity employment goals! I think you need to just shut up and mind your own business."*

Glen (after 5 seconds of silence): *"I have heard that, but that's not the issue."*

Bob: *"It's the issue to me! You work hard all your life and hope that you will be appreciated, then realize that management doesn't care and performance doesn't matter. You're just a number on a profile. Don't you get frustrated?"*

Glen: *"Yes, but that's not the issue right now."*

Bob (significantly less angry): *"So, what is the issue?"*

Glen (softer voice): *"Let me repeat, I need you to exhibit a more positive attitude during work hours; by that I mean, if you have a problem with another person or group, going to that person or group to address the issue instead of talking negatively about them in public or behind their back to other staff. Also, if you do, I will have more respect for you and there will be a more positive team atmosphere."*

Bob (indignant): *"You're asking me to not say anything negative about anyone? That's absurd—not humanly possible!"*

Glen: *"Yes, that's what I'm asking."*

Bob (calmer): *"All the guys enjoy our stories, it relieves the stress. It's not just me, everyone feels the same. Are you going to bug everyone?"*

Glen: *Yes, rest assured that, if I have this issue with anyone else, I will go to that person, in private, with the same request."*

Bob: *"Don't you think you are overstepping your bounds? You are not my boss."*

Glen: *"No, I'm not your boss, and no, I'm not beyond my bounds."*

Bob (laughing tensely): *"You're goofy! You will never make it here. No way!"*

Glenn: *"I'm going to take your response as a 'no.' The consequence of you not being willing to change is that I'm going to hand in my resignation and, as an explanation for why, I will, in writing, indicate that your negative behavior is the reason."*

Bob: *"That's a threat! That's blackmail! Management won't do anything about it anyway!"*

Glen: *"No, it's not a threat. It's that important to me!"*

Bob: *"You really mean this then? You would quit over this?"*

Glen: *"Yes!"*

Bob (with lowered voice): *"Listen, you are a good guy. I didn't mean any harm. I have always been too opinionated, even my wife tells me so. I don't think I can change overnight and I like gossip."*

Glen: *"Gossip is OK. I'm asking that it not include negative judgments or prejudicial remarks about people."*

Bob: *"Is that even possible?"*

Glen: *"Yes, over time if you are willing to change. I will even help. If you slip, I will remind you in private so you are aware when it happens."*

Bob: *"OK, I'll try. So you won't quit."*

Glen: *"No, I won't quit if you do this. I appreciate your agreeing to change."*

Bob: *"I'm sorry."*

Glen: *"Thanks."*

How did you respond to these sample confrontations? Comfortable or a bit uneasy? They are both quite direct and assertive, and contain a high level of control of the influencing process. Yet both worked—they resulted in a behavior change, were not hurtful, and were not allowed to become conflict.

Both of the people reported that they were apprehensive at the start, but quite relaxed when finished. Both people felt compassion and empathy, but not guilt. Both also reported that the relationship with the person they confronted improved.

There is no one right or wrong way to confront or influence. You need to use influencing options that are consistent with your values. Hopefully, you are now more aware that there are several ways to confront and that each, based on the words and tone, has its own predictable impact on the other person. It's your choice!

Yet, if you use the skills presented in this book, you can confront without getting into conflict and without having to feel guilty about having been hurtful.

Epilogue

Life is a series of choices. At each choice point, effective people have options. They take responsibility for their choices and do not blame the world.

Having the skill to be able to confront effectively, without creating conflict, is but one of many necessary life skills. Yet, for those of us who value our quality of life, it is critical. Without the option to confront, we may be choosing to be reactive, passive or powerless.

It is my hope that you have gained some clarity about the options you already have and will find this new confrontation option helpful. Use it wisely and with integrity.

APPENDIX A

Confrontation for Supervisors

A critical part of your job as a supervisor is to have all employees performing to standards consistently on every aspect of their job. If they are meeting standards, you should give positive feedback. If they are not, you are required to request that they do so. If you do not confront (request that performance be up to standards), you are not doing your supervisory job!

Therefore, to decide whether to confront is not an option!

If performance is meeting standards, you are getting a "yes." If performance is not meeting standards, you are getting a "no" at the moment. Your job is to up the level of control as soon as possible.

You have probably heard the terms "coaching" and "counseling." Both involve respectfully discussing the performance issue with the employee, with the goal of solving the performance problem. If you have discussed and oriented the employee to the specific performance standards, this coaching or counseling can begin with the soft, low-risk Discrepancy Confrontation.

Examples:

"I'm confused because, on the one hand, you clearly understood the standards, while on the other hand, performance is not to the standard."

"I'm concerned because, on the one hand, you have performed this task (define) to standard in the past, while on the other hand, performance is not to standard recently."

If you have not previously been clear with or discussed the specific standards, you should confront using the Behavior Request Confrontation so that the performance standards are clear. In this case, the standard is the behavior that you are requesting.

Example:
> *"I need you to _____(specific desired behavior)_____, and as a result,*
> *_____(consequences)_____."*

Regardless of which confontation format you use to address the issue, if performance improves, you are getting a "yes." If performance does not improve, you are getting a "no" and have to up the level of control by using a stronger confrontation, negotiating, and/or describing the consequences (moving from positive to negative).

Often, supervisors procrastinate or avoid confronting difficult performance issues. If you delay, the performance problem continues and usually gets worse, you build up excess emotional baggage, and it negatively impacts or demotivates other staff members.

If you are unable to address performance issues quickly, I suggest establishing a systematic performance feedback process. Such a process will ensure that performance issues are confronted.

A systematic feedback process involves giving feedback on a regularly scheduled basis, such as once per month, the time frame being tailored to your business situation.

During this short meeting, both you and the employee discuss one or two positive performance accomplishments and one or two areas where the employee wants or needs to improve. When you discuss these areas needing improvement, you use a Behavior Request.

Once you have requested and agreed upon an area of improvement, be sure to develop a plan for accomplishing the desired improvement. I have included a sample Growth Plan that many of my clients use (Figure A-1). You might find it useful to consider the changing behavior strategies outlined in Chapter 10 when developing a Growth Plan.

Growth Plan

Employee Name

Date

Action I Will Take	By: (Date)	Follow-up I Will Take	By: (Date)	Results/Behavior Expected	By: (Date)

Supervisor Name

Date

Action I Will Take	By: (Date)	Follow-up I Will Take	By: (Date)	Results/Behavior Expected	By: (Date)

Figure A-1

APPENDIX B

Worksheets

The following worksheets are duplicates of those contained in the book and are for your use.

Behavior Request Confrontation Worksheet

1. Describe the person's undesirable behavior (what she/he is doing that is causing you a problem).

   _____

   _____

   _____

2. What do you want the person to do? (the opposite of what you don't like)

   I would like him/her to: _____

   _____

   _____

3. Add specificity (if what you are requesting is described with a non-specific term, add specificity).

   I would like you to _____

   _____

   by that I mean _____

   _____

   or, for example _____

   _____

   or, as demonstrated by _____

   _____

   or, more specifically _____

   _____

4. Add the positive consequences if she/he changes.

   . . . and, as a result, if you do, _____

   _____

   _____

   _____

Behavior Request Confrontation Worksheet

1. Describe the person's undesirable behavior (what she/he is doing that is causing you a problem).

    _____

    _____

    _____

2. What do you want the person to do? (the opposite of what you don't like)

    I would like him/her to: _____

    _____

    _____

    _____

3. Add specificity (if what you are requesting is described with a non-specific term, add specificity).

    I would like you to _____

    _____

    by that I mean _____

    _____

    or, for example _____

    _____

    or, as demonstrated by _____

    _____

    or, more specifically _____

    _____

4. Add the positive consequences if she/he changes.

    . . . and, as a result, if you do, _____

    _____

    _____

    _____

Discrepancy Confrontation Worksheet

Using the same issue you used when you wrote your Behavior Request Confrontation, write a Discrepancy Confrontation:

I feel _____because on the one hand
        (1) (your feeling)

_____ ,
        (2) (positive attribute of the person)

while on the other hand, _____

_____ ,
        (3) (undesirable behavior)

_____ .

Discrepancy Confrontation Worksheet

Using the same issue you used when you wrote your Behavior Request Confrontation, write a Discrepancy Confrontation:

I feel _____because on the one hand
        (1) (your feeling)

_____ ,
        (2) (positive attribute of the person)

while on the other hand, _____

_____ ,
        (3) (undesirable behavior)

_____ .

Accountability Confrontation Worksheet

Write an Accountability Confrontation using the same issue you used in Figure 6-7 and Figure 6-9:

"*I* _____

(1) (degree of control/choice word)

to know if you are willing to _____

_____ '*yes*' *or* '*no*'?"

(2) (specific behavior)

_____ '*yes*' *or* '*no*'?"

Accountability Confrontation Worksheet

Write an Accountability Confrontation using the same issue you used in Figure 6-7 and Figure 6-9:

"*I* _____

(1) (degree of control/choice word)

to know if you are willing to _____

_____ '*yes*' *or* '*no*'?"

(2) (specific behavior)

_____ '*yes*' *or* '*no*'?"

Confrontation Strategy Worksheet

1. What Do I Want? *(Write your request in a Behavior Request Confrontation format):*

   I _____

      (degree of control/choice word or phrase)

   you to _____

      (desired behavior with specificity)

   _____

   _____

   _____

   and, as a result _____

   _____

      (consequence/result)

2. Is It Worth Doing? ❏ Yes ❏ No

3. What's the WPPSS/Risk? _____

   _____

   (a) Is the WPPSS Real? ❏ Yes ❏ No   (b) Can I Live With This Risk? ❏ Yes ❏ No

4. What Am I Going to Do If I Get a "No?" _____

   _____

5. At What Confrontation Level Am I Going to Begin?

   ❏ Discrepancy ❏ Behavior Request ❏ Accountability

6. Do I Have Specific Facts or Examples of the Undesirable Behavior If Needed?

   1. _____

   2. _____

7. What "No" Behavior Do I Expect?

   ❏ Anger ❏ Blaming ❏ Confusion ❏ Hurt ❏ Silence ❏ Others _____

8. How Will I Respond to This Expected "No" Behavior? _____

9. How Much Time Will I Spend With This "No" Behavior? _____

10. What Confrontation or "No" Strategy Will I Move to If I Get a "No" to My Initial

    Confrontation? _____

11. Will Putting My Confrontation into Context Help?

    ❏ Yes ❏ No

12. Am I Confronting the Right Person First?

    ❏ Yes ❏ No

    If Not, Who or Which People Do I Need to Confront First? _____

Confrontation Strategy Worksheet

1. What Do I Want? *(Write your request in a Behavior Request Confrontation format):*

   I _____

   (degree of control/choice word or phrase)

   you to _____

   (desired behavior with specificity)

   _____

   _____

   _____

   _____

   and, as a result _____

   _____

   (consequence/result)

2. Is It Worth Doing? ❑ Yes ❑ No

3. What's the WPPSS/Risk? _____

   _____

   (a) Is the WPPSS Real? ❑ Yes ❑ No   (b) Can I Live With This Risk? ❑ Yes ❑ No

4. What Am I Going to Do If I Get a "No?" _____

   _____

5. At What Confrontation Level Am I Going to Begin?

   ❑ Discrepancy ❑ Behavior Request ❑ Accountability

6. Do I Have Specific Facts or Examples of the Undesirable Behavior If Needed?

   1. _____

   2. _____

7. What "No" Behavior Do I Expect?

   ❑ Anger ❑ Blaming ❑ Confusion ❑ Hurt ❑ Silence ❑ Others _____

8. How Will I Respond to This Expected "No" Behavior? _____

9. How Much Time Will I Spend With This "No" Behavior? _____

10. What Confrontation or "No" Strategy Will I Move to If I Get a "No" to My Initial

    Confrontation? _____

11. Will Putting My Confrontation into Context Help?

    ❑ Yes ❑ No

12. Am I Confronting the Right Person First?

    ❑ Yes ❑ No

    If Not, Who or Which People Do I Need to Confront First? _____

References

Berenson, Bernard G., and Carkhuff, Robert R. *Sources of gain in Counseling & Psychotherapy.* New York: Holt, Rinehart & Winston, Inc., 1967.

Berenson, B. G., and Mitchell, K. M. *Confrontation: For Better or Worse.* Amherst, MA: Human Resource Development Press, 1974.

Bernstein, A. J., and Craft Rozen, Sidney. *Dinosaur Brains.* New York: John Wiley & Sons, Inc., 1989.

Bradshaw, John. *Healing the Shame That Binds You.* Deerfield Beach, FL: Health Communications, Inc., 1988.

Carkhuff, Robert R. *The Art of Helping.* Amherst, MA: Human Resource Development Press, 1987.

Carkhuff, Robert R., and Berenson, B. G. *Beyond Counseling and Therapy.* New York: Holt, Rinehart & Winston, 1977.

Covey, Stephen R. *The Seven Habits of Highly Effective People.* New York: Fireside, Simon and Schuster, 1989.

Dreikurs, R. & Cassel, P. *Discipline Without Tears.* 2nd Edition. New York: Hawthorn Books, 1972.

Gordon, Thomas. *Parent Effectiveness Training.* New York: Peter H. Wyden, 1972.

Peter, L. G. *The Peter Principle.* William Morrow, 1969.

Index

My goal is to provide "hands-on" skills that work!

Since I too have a mutual goal of growth and improvement, I would appreciate your feedback about this book, including ways it might be improved. Please send feedback to:

Bob Weyant
Bob Weyant & Associates
P. O. Box 6414
Bellevue, WA 98008-0414
(425) 747-4898
Fax: (425) 747-0724

I provide consulting, training, and speaking services to organizations. If you would like further information regarding my services or would like additional copies of this book, please call or write to me at the above address.

Book Order Form

Telephone Orders: (425) 747-4898

Fax Orders: (425) 747-0724, fill out the order blank and fax.

Postal Orders: Fill out the order blank and mail to:

Bob Weyant
P.O. Box 6414
Bellevue, WA 98008-0414

Ship To:

Company Name _____

Name _____

Address _____

_____

City _____ State _____

Zip _____ Phone _____

Confronting Without Guilt or Conflict	U.S. Price	Total Price
Quantity:	$19.95	
Over 10 Books/Less 10%		
Subtotal		
WA State Residents Add 8.6% Sales Tax		
Shipping/Handling* (Within U.S. add $3.00 for one book, $1.00 for each additional book) * For international orders, call for rate.		
TOTAL ENCLOSED		

Thank you for your order!

I understand that I may return any book for a full refund if not satisfied.